Our Dear Sandra & Gary,

May the Lord give you strength to face each day and assurance of His divine presence to sustain you.

We ♡ you both & all the kids as well. We are here to help & serve you. Please try us anytime.

Presented To:

Gary & Sandra Pelaez

From:

Jose & Sonia Flores

Date:

April 8th 2003

Peace in the Midst of the Storm

by

Zada Sherry

RIVER
OAK
PUBLISHING

Tulsa, Oklahoma

Peace in the Midst of the Storm
ISBN 1-58919-632-5
Copyright © 2001 by Zada Sherry

Published by RiverOak Publishing
P.O. Box 700143
Tulsa, Oklahoma 74170-0143

In Memory of Paul

Who taught my heart to sing
And to the honor and glory of God
Who gave me the song.

Acknowledgments

My grateful appreciation must go to the special women, without whom the task of transforming my journal into a manuscript would never have been attempted or completed—Elsie Miller, Brenda Partain, Kathy Myers, Helen Carraker, and Jan Hubbard. I would also like to thank their husbands and families for their patience and understanding. And my special thanks to Sandy Gearhart, who prepared the first manuscript for critiquing.

I am deeply appreciative to Craig Newhouse, for his timely advice, generosity, and prayerful support. Also my gratitude to Liz, his wife, for her prayers and support, and Don Newhouse, who gave of his time and facilities.

Perhaps the ones to whom I am most indebted are the silent, dedicated individuals who were always in the background, undergirding this project with their prayers. There are too many to list here, but they know who they are, and to them goes my heartfelt thanks. Whatever good may result from this work is due to these dear friends, and most of all to the Holy Spirit who was the source of it all, and who is always at work in the midst of us.

Foreword

Seldom does one have the privilege of walking intimately with a fellow human being through suffering and heartbreak. In fact, such fellowship is hardly on the list of priorities for those who like stories that end, "and they lived happily ever after."

But Zada Sherry has described her journey through sorrow in such a way as to reveal it to be a venture borne on eagle's wings. Not without tears, not without moments of darkness, but always with a song—even in the longest hours of the night.

I am glad God let me walk part of the way with her.

T. Ervin Veale, B.D.

Introduction

I began the journal from which this book has been taken on New Year's Eve 1966. I desired it to be my "love song to God," written out of the everyday experiences of a simple woman who happened to be married to a minister. I had no hint at that time of the difficult journey ahead of me, or the wonderful lessons God would teach me along the way. I did have a strong compulsion to be persistent and faithful in recording, not only the lessons I was learning, but also my emotions and feelings as the events occurred. It seemed important that I be as honest and transparent as possible.

Looking back on the two years I kept the journal, it seems almost incredible that I was able to chronicle the events which were happening. At that time, it felt as if I had no choice. It was something I had to do and it did not seem difficult. Rather, the writing brought me strength and courage. As I wrote I learned many things about myself and about God. It is, of course, not possible to include two years of entries in a book of regular size. Therefore, I have carefully selected the very best of what I have learned and experienced. These I now pass on to you with great joy.

Zada Sherry

December 31, 1965

One thing I ask of the LORD, this is what I seek:
that I may dwell in the house of the LORD
all the days of my life, to gaze upon the beauty
of the LORD and to seek him in his temple.

—PSALM 27:4

This is New Year's Eve! I am beginning the new year propped up in bed, learning to write for the first time with my left hand. My right arm, badly injured last October, is in a heavy cast. I can most assuredly identify with the feelings of the Psalmist, who once cried: *Be merciful to me, LORD, for I am faint; O LORD, heal me, for my bones are in agony* (Psalms 6:2). This has been a trying and difficult experience for me, one that has required great patience and dependence upon God.

Lying here tonight, listening to the bells and whistles heralding the new year, I have had a sudden strong desire to keep a journal. I would like it to be my "love song" to God, written out of my own daily experiences. God is the source of all music. I shall offer Him the words—the music must be His.

O God, my Father, it is my prayer, at the beginning of this new year, that I may be protected from all those things which would grieve You and be enabled, by Your grace, to do all the things which would please You and bring joy to Your heart. Amen.

January 3, 1966

Answer me when I call to you, O my righteous God.
Give me relief from my distress;
be merciful to me and hear my prayer.

—PSALM 4:1

God stretches us, I am discovering, during times of stress. I am making new discoveries about patience. It seems to be the outer evidence of my inner knowledge and relationship with God. The more fully I know Him, the more completely my soul rests in patience because I am learning to trust Him. I can rest in His arms when storms rage, when my future is uncertain, when my body is sick or in pain.

I wonder if I can rejoice and praise God now, even in my pain and disability. I want to! Because I love Him. And, at the present time, there is not much else I can do for Him. So praising Him seems to be an obvious way to show Him my devotion.

Teach me, Lord, through my pain. Help me to learn
the lessons You have for me and to come to know
You better. May I learn to share more deeply
in the fellowship of the world's suffering. Amen.

 *January 25, 1966*

As thy days, so shall thy strength be.

—DEUTERONOMY 33:25 KJV

How many days do I have left in my life? Only God knows. My times are in His hands. No matter how long or how short the time may be, no matter how much I desire to accomplish in my lifetime, the frailties of my flesh make me totally dependent upon Him. I really have no life in myself. Our brother James was thinking of this when he wrote, *What is your life? You are a mist that appears for a little while and then vanishes* (James 4:14 KJV).

Our Lord gives us the assurance, however, that we shall have sufficient strength for each one of our days. What a wonder! What "amazing grace" is this! I need not fear the future, then, for in the times of my greatest weakness He will be present with His strength. As my days . . . so shall His strength be in me!

*I place myself and all my days into Your hands,
dear Father. Thank You for giving me the strength
I need for each day. I will look to You in my weakness,
trusting the faithfulness of Your love for me. Amen.*

February 2, 1966

*Out of the depths I cry to you, O L*ORD.
—PSALM 130:1

I have read this scripture many times, but for the first time it has found a response in my own soul. It does not take a major crisis to evoke such a feeling—a dark and crushing valley of despair. Instead, I sometimes think these words may find their response as easily in the midst of frustration, monotony, and the sheer nothingness of a desert crossing. Did the psalmist, perhaps, utter this cry in a moment of boredom?

I often hear the lament: "But I am not *doing* anything! Life is so daily—every day the same—nothing *really* happens." I am coming to see more and more clearly, and experiencing in my own life, that God does some of His deepest and most important work in us during times of loneliness and spiritual dryness.

*Dear God, I give You praise that You have an answer
for all of my needs. Whether I am walking through
a dry and barren desert or the valley of the shadow of
death, You are with me, comforting, guiding, strengthening.
My heart is grateful for Your caring. Amen.*

February 9, 1966

Give unto the LORD the glory due unto His name; worship
the LORD in the beauty of holiness.

—PSALM 29:2 KJV

My thoughts today are drawn to Mary of Bethany as
she sat at the feet of Jesus, listening to Him speak and
getting to know Him better. I wonder when it was that she
realized He would soon die. She certainly knew when she
poured precious ointment over His feet. Jesus understood
perfectly why she had done this, and that she had saved the
ointment for that very purpose. He told those who
watched that she had kept it to anoint Him for His burial.
Mary's gift was the only preparation for death He received!
As she wiped His feet with her hair, her own person took
on the very fragrance of the Lord!

In that future day when we bow before Him, the
Bible says, *we shall be like him* (1 John 3:2). I am
delighted by that image—the magnificent promise of
seeing Him face to face and being like Him. What a
wonderful day that will be!

> *Teach me, Lord, to sit quietly at Your feet—*
> *listening, learning as Mary did. So that even now*
> *I may offer my gift of praise and give forth*
> *the sweet fragrance of Your person. Amen.*

February 14, 1966

The LORD appeared to us in the past, saying:
"I have loved you with an everlasting love;
I have drawn you with loving-kindness."

—JEREMIAH 31:3

This is Valentine's Day. On this special day, I am so grateful for God's love. I am also grateful for my precious husband, Paul, my earthly companion and friend. To walk by his side in ministry is my joy and privilege.

Our marriage has not always been what it is now. When Paul and I first married, we were deeply in love and blissfully absorbed with each other. But the day came when the serpent entered our paradise. Storms of destruction rolled across our Eden. When they passed we looked at each other and it seemed there was nothing left between us but desolation and ruin.

It was then that two broken individuals knelt before their Maker and offered back to Him their shattered, rebellious lives. With warm and tender hands, God took the broken pieces and recreated them. We placed our lives and our marriage in the hands of the Potter and were made whole.

Thank You, Father, for the revelation of Your amazing love for me. Thank You also for Your great healing and restoration, and the love my husband brings to my life. I will cherish both with new zeal from this day forward. Amen.

February 23, 1966

" . . .They will call him Immanuel"—
which means, "God with us."

—MATTHEW 1:23

This statement excites my deepest awe, and challenges my most thoughtful attention. Reduced to its basic simplicity it means that God cared enough to become involved in the miserable and tragic result of man's rebellion against Him. Such graciousness is beyond my comprehension.

The law indeed came by Moses, but grace and truth by Jesus Christ (John 1:17). He came so graciously and willingly, bringing—and being—the Truth. Jesus Christ is God's Truth to light our way home to the Father's house. He came not only to show us the way, but to also accompany us on the journey. For He is God . . . with us.

Send forth your light and your truth, let them guide me; let them bring me to your holy mountain, to the place where you dwell (Psalm 43:3).

*Lord, thank you for leaving the Father, shedding
your wondrous royalty, to come and live among men. Thank
you for humbling yourself to a natural death—and yet
unnatural as you took the sins of men, the true weight of the
world, onto your divine shoulders.
And thank you for being "God with us," even now.*

February 28, 1966

*After Job had prayed for his friends,
the LORD made him prosperous again and
gave him twice as much as he had before.*

—JOB 42:10

Paul and I went to the convalescent home today. While he was visiting with a patient, I walked into another room and prayed with a woman I knew. Later, while talking with her, I realized that I had been freed from fears and inhibitions that had previously kept me ineffectual in my ministry to others. Part of the "self" life that had been a hindrance to me was a spirit of timidity, inferiority, and self-consciousness. Because of the nature of my work with Paul, not many would have suspected that I had such a problem. For me it was very real.

I cannot explain how I became aware of my new freedom. I became aware of a real caring for the patient . . . an empathy with her and a compassion, which was new for me. It is not always easy to understand, or to verbalize what is transpiring in one's spirit.

*I thank You, Lord, that You help Your children grow.
Continue to stretch me, that I may be a true
servant of You and Your people. Amen.*

March 2, 1966

Why then is it written that the Son of Man must suffer much and be rejected?

—MARK 9:12

Through these words, and other passages of scripture, we come to understand that Jesus Christ was made as nothing, that we might become the sons and daughters of the most high God. He was utterly despised, so that we might be made the elect of God, holy and beloved. He made Himself of no reputation, so that we might become partakers of the divine nature. For our sakes He became poor, in order that we might have an inheritance incorruptible and undefiled, one which is reserved in heaven for us and does not fade away.

We exchange everything that makes us miserable and unhappy for that which will bring us fulfillment and joy. We exchange slavery for freedom, ashes for beauty, mourning for joy, the spirit of heaviness for the spirit of praise.

Jesus, who, being in very nature God, did not consider equality with God something to be grasped, but made Himself nothing and became obedient to death—even death on a cross!

Lord, I am humbled by this concept, this reality and can scarcely take it in. Please give me a spirit of meekness and humility as I walk this earth. Words cannot express my gratitude for Your sacrifice.

March 6, 1966

"Forsake all and thou shalt find rest."

—THOMAS A KEMPIS

This statement brings me to confront my priorities. Where are my values? Is there anything I cannot give up, anything I can't live without? As long as I am clinging to things—no matter how good or lawful—I delay the spiritual riches that are awaiting me. God cannot pour His riches into hands that are already full.

Yet, even here we need God's help. The world has such a strong hold that it takes more than mere desire to relinquish our grip. We clutch our possessions; afraid to let them go, afraid to trust God. He does not want to strip us of the things we possess . . . only of their possession of us.

He longs for our hearts to be fully committed to Him, so that He can pour out on our lives all the gifts and privileges of His kingdom.

Father, You said You wished that we were either hot or cold. You hate lukewarmness. Please make me a flame, Lord, that I may burn for You alone. Amen.

*You care for the land and water it; you enrich it
abundantly. The streams of God are filled with water
to provide the people with grain, for so you have ordained
it. The meadows are covered with flocks and the valleys
are mantled with grain; they shout for joy and sing.*

—PSALM 65:9,13

It is Spring! Winter is over! The birds are trilling their
joy. Flowers of the early springtime are parading a rainbow
of colors on every lawn, and their intoxicating fragrance is
wafted on every breeze. Overhead, the sky . . . the blue,
blue sky . . . and the flocks of angel clouds lift the soul
heavenward. My soul sings a hymn of praise:

God . . . how great You are! How wondrous are Your
ways! All this, the work of Your mighty hands. But You
are even greater than Your works! My soul melts, O God,
in adoration of You. And yet You say: *I live in a high and
holy place, but also with him who is contrite and lowly in
spirit* (Isaiah 57:15).

*I am amazed when I think of all Your facets, Lord,
Your great vastness—and how You, the powerful Creator,
became my Savior! I'm in awe of this realization!*

April 5, 1966

Bless the Lord, O my soul and all that is within me, bless His holy name.

—PSALM 103:1 KJV

To worship and adore You with all my being, as these words indicate, is my deepest desire and my prayer. But how do I do it, Lord? My capacity seems so small, my talents limited. Even my love for You is weak and vacillating. In other words, I am a shallow vessel! What can I do, Lord? Please teach me what I need to know.

The chambered nautilus leaves its old shell upon the sandy shore to exchange it for a new one. Is that what Heaven will be like? To exchange my little self for a larger capacity to worship You? Will eternity be growth in knowledge of You, so that I can more perfectly love You and magnify Your holy name?

Yes, that's it. Even as I am writing, You are teaching me about praise. The composer may bring You his music, the artist his painting, but it is praise which delights Your heart and this, every person may give You. I am beginning to understand that praise is a divine drill— enlarging us, making the well of the soul deeper, to contain Your Living Water!

Receive, dear Lord, my song of love and praise.
May all that is within me give You praise.

April 13, 1966

> *He gathers the waters of the sea into jars;*
> *he puts the deep into storehouses.*
>
> —PSALM 33:7

Paul has been very tired the last few weeks, and we have come to this lovely island for a few days of rest. We are in a little cabin on the Gulf, provided for us by our son Kenneth, who brought us here this morning. He ate lunch with us, then returned home.

Now we are alone with God and each other! The mysteries of the sea and sky speak to our hearts of the revelations of God yet awaiting us. We are here by His appointment, to meet Him and to be taught of Him. Last night, God's instructions to me for the coming days seemed to be:

"Begin to listen more. Become increasingly still within, and attend to each individual, and every interruption, or providence, as thought it were of the utmost importance, as indeed it is. See Me in everything and do not be impatient or restive under restrictions, changed plans, dull conversations, or thwarted purposes.

"Learn to watch for My opening doors. Consider every person of equal importance; any location as the place where I desire you to be at that moment. Learn the discipline of attentiveness and the importance of the listening ear. Be more sensitive to the gentle spirit . . . the timid soul . . . and the hungry hearts of those to whom you minister."

I wait before You, O God!

April 17, 1966

*What shall I render unto the Lord
for all His benefits toward me?*

—PSALM 116:12 KJV

This is the anniversary of the day, an Easter Sunday night, when she came to us! You sent Kathy, Father . . . this lovely daughter of ours . . . knowing how much we needed her then, how empty our lives would have been without her . . . and how much we were going to need her.

On this anniversary of the day of her birth, I give this page of my journal to praise You for the gift of her life. You entrusted her to us, but she is Yours. Though she is an adult with a family of her own, I continue to pray for her.

For her warm, unfailing love and faith in us, I praise You. For her love and devotion to You, I praise You more! For her place in Your purposes I shall praise You forever. May she give Your strength, comfort, and love to every life she touches, even as she does to ours. Protect her and her loved ones, O God, from Satan's power, that they may be preserved for Your highest and most holy purposes forever. Amen.

# *April 19, 1966*

SOUTH PADRE ISLAND

But the wicked are like the tossing sea, which cannot rest, whose waves cast up mire and mud. "There is no peace," says my God, "for the wicked."

—ISAIAH 57:20-21

God has promised in His Word that there is a rest for His people. But people living without God are like the restless, troubled waves that pound against this island.

The Lord Jesus Christ is that rest for the Christian. When we come to know Him, we understand the meaning of His loving invitation; *Come unto Me, all ye that labor and are heavy laden, and I will give you rest* (Matthew 11:28 KJV).

St. Jude describes people who live without God as wandering stars—out of orbit. God, in His mercy and love, has made provision to get us back in orbit when we get out of it; to make of us gentle breezes of blessing; rain clouds of refreshment to others.

Once I was part of that empty, restless world. Once I also beat in futility against the shores of God's immovable, holy will. Now I can humbly say that, not through any righteousness of my own, but because of His grace and mercy, I have found His rest.

Thank You for the hope I have which allows me to experience peace and rest, even in times of trouble and testing. Thank You for taking my burdens, dear Lord.

April 20, 1966

SOUTH PADRE ISLAND

Deep calls to deep in the roar of your waterfalls;
all your waves and breakers have swept over me.

—PSALM 42:7

Yesterday afternoon the fog rolled in over our island. We walked along the shore hand in hand, and then stood silently looking out into the mist. We could scarcely see the separation between the sea and the fog. They became as one. It was exhilarating! We walked through the fog, watching the white froth of the waves beating against the jetties. Our hair and clothing were soaked, as though we were walking in the rain. The sea and the fog appeared to be as one because the nature of them was the same.

So it is in our relationship with You, O God! Deep calleth to deep . . . Spirit to spirit. The sailor hears the voice of the sea because he has the love of the sea in his heart. The child of God responds to the call of God because he has taken the very nature of God.

It is only when we have become one with You and the
troubled waves of life roll over us, that we know and
recognize them to be the "fathomless billows" of Your love.

April 25, 1966

> *But this is what the LORD says: "Yes, captives*
> *will be taken from warriors, and plunder*
> *retrieved from the fierce; I will contend with those*
> *who contend with you, and your children I will save.*

—ISAIAH 49:25

We are at Kenneth's home tonight, on our way back to Oklahoma. We have spent the evening visiting with him and his family. After returning to our room, I opened my Bible to this special verse of scripture. It suddenly became significant.

It is my prayer, Father, that our children, grandchildren, and all of our descendants shall be Yours without the loss of one. May they all be builders in Your Kingdom. Protect them, I pray, even against their own desires, when at any time those desires are contrary to Your divine will for them. Teach them Your ways, and may those ways be their delight and joy.

Father, I thank You for our children and grandchildren, and for the hours You have given us to be with them. They enrich our lives. Watch over them and guide their paths. Establish each one of them in Your salvation and in Your peace, for Your dear Son's sake. Amen.

May 3, 1966

> *We demolish arguments and every pretension that*
> *sets itself up against the knowledge of God, and we take*
> *captive every thought to make it obedient to Christ.*

—2 CORINTHIANS 10:5

My God, I come to You tonight in gratitude and fullness of heart. I am grateful, beyond words, for all that You are to me, through me and in me. I am grateful for all You have done, are now doing, and will continue to do for me. You have indeed become my Lord. Anything within me that would defy You, or take preeminence over Your Lordship is offensive to me. You are in the process of forming me into Your likeness because I have given You permission to do so. I trust You, Lord, to complete that work in my life. Because I am often willful and rebellious, Your pressure at times causes me pain. Sometimes I resist You, and occasionally I actively refuse to respond to You.

The enemy attacks me in my thought life. He knows my weaknesses and attacks me with incredible accuracy. These are areas where I must totally depend upon You, because I can't overcome these prideful, vain imaginations in my own strength.

> *Lord, Your word says You will complete Your work in me.*
> *I open myself to that work and ask that You help me to*
> *become more like Christ in all aspects of life. Thank You.*

27

" . . . He is Lord of lords and King of kings—and with him will be his called, chosen, and faithful followers."

—Revelation 17:14

These words: *called . . . chosen . . . faithful . . .* describe a true follower of the Lord Jesus Christ. They speak of discipleship. My thoughts seem to focus upon the word *faithful . . .* one of the great attributes of God. Moses describes Him as a faithful God. On the other hand, one of the dominant characteristics of the Israelites was their tendency to be unfaithful in their covenant relationship with God. Fidelity is such an important attribute for growth. It determines whether we will make progress in our walk with Him, or will remain paralyzed and motionless.

It is often through our human relationships that we learn faithfulness toward God. If we are not true to one another we may be certain there will be areas of instability in our relationship with Him.

I must begin with God on the basis of openness and honesty, no matter what my spiritual condition, and He will take me from there. It helps me to remember that nothing in my nature is shocking to God. It may surprise *us* to discover what we are like, but God has always known. He wants us to know too, so that we can grow.

Help me, Lord, to be faithful.
Help me to be honest with myself—and You.

May 9, 1966

Love is patient, love is kind. It does not envy, it does not boast, it is not proud. It always protects, always trusts, always hopes, always perseveres. Love never fails.

—1 CORINTHIANS 13:4,7,8

Paul and I need more love and compassion in our lives and ministry! Last night, God seemed to show me this church, and its people, in a way I had never seen. Almost every family in our church is bearing some kind of burden or heartache. God unfolded their needs before me one by one, as a long unwinding reel.

In that moment I realized that pastors and other Christian leaders often forget, or are insensitive to, the pain experienced by their people. Financial difficulties, family problems, loneliness, sickness—all are a part of the church family life. It is easy to expect too much. Not everyone has been called to a pastoral vocation, but they are no less dear or important to God.

When the heart is breaking, words—even good words—sometimes fall on deaf ears. They can beat on defenseless heads, almost like blows. And they are unheard. I know . . . I remember. For once, I was among those who hurt too deeply to hear. However, the *heart* hears the voice of love—without words—and responds.

Father, show us how to see people with the eyes of the heart . . . to express Your love to others.

> *I will not sacrifice to the LORD my God*
> *burnt offerings that cost me nothing.*

—2 SAMUEL 24:24

It cost God everything to purchase our salvation and provide for our eternal life with Him. He gave His Son. No other sacrifice could assure man's salvation. The value of this gift is beyond human comprehension.

In a similar manner, God esteems our gifts and offerings to Him by what they cost us. My tears, struggles, and pain—even my bitter defeats are known to Him. The Psalmist tells us that God is aware of our tears. Sometimes we have nothing else to give Him except our tears, and we can be assured, if that is the case, they are not unnoticed by God.

There are, to be sure, shallow tears of self-pity, which spring from self-indulgence. But there are also tears of intercession for others, tears that spring from the anguish of repentance or sorrow, and there are tears, which come from a heart overflowing with adoration and praise. They are the very essence of ourselves, and can be our supreme gift to Him! Such tears are of inestimable significance and value to God.

> *Father, I want to thank You because You do not*
> *despise the least of our gifts. Thank you for one*
> *more glimpse into Your heart and character.*

May 13, 1966

Those whom I love I rebuke and discipline. So be earnest, and repent.

—REVELATION 3:19

When we give ourselves to God, He commits Himself to us, with the assurance that *He is able to keep us from falling and to present us faultless before the presence of His glory with exceeding joy"* (Jude 24 KJV). This will be a time of rejoicing when we see our Lord face to face, and enter into the joys He has prepared for those who love Him.

He has been exceedingly patient with me. He has lifted me when I have fallen, dusted me off, wiped away my tears, comforted me when I have disappointed Him (as well as myself). The day will come when all this will be over. He will take my hand and present me to His Father. I can almost hear His words: "Here is Zada, Father. I have had a difficult time with her. She has often been willful and rebellious, but I have brought her safely into Your Kingdom." I believe Jude is telling me that Jesus will do this with great joy!

Father, help me to submit willingly to Your discipline.
You have come to me as a refiner of silver.
Thank You, Father, for Your loving correction.

 *May 21, 1966*

*I urge you to keep up your courage, because not
one of you will be lost. . . . Last night an angel
of the God whose I am and whom I serve stood
beside me and said, "Do not be afraid, Paul.
You must stand trial before Caesar; and God has
graciously given you the lives of all who sail with you.*

—ACTS 27:22-24

Someone has said that in this life we are like "ships
that pass in the night." What a blessed assurance it would
be to know that, as in the above scripture, all who "sail
with us" would be given to us, for God.

We pass them every day—little ships on the troubled
waters of life. Their sails are flapping in the wind . . . their
rudders broken . . . and some are grounded and completely
helpless. We call to them across the waves. We nod and
smile encouragement. We point to the harbor . . . with
calm and safety waiting so close at hand! But they do not
see us, nor do they hear our voices. The roaring wind, the
tossing waves, their battered and broken vessels have all
their attention. They do not see the stars above them,
shining through the broken clouds of night.

*Help me to know how to speak to people who are
hurting. Open their eyes, O Lord, to see You walking
toward them across the waves with outstretched arms,
saying, "Be not afraid; it is I."*

May 26, 1966

*I know, O LORD, that a man's life is not his own; it is
not for man to direct his steps. Correct me, LORD,
but only with justice—not in your anger,
lest you reduce me to nothing.*

—JEREMIAH 10:23-24

The words "direct his steps" catch my attention.
Walking was a mode of travel in the days of Jesus. He
spent much of His time walking, and as He did, He
ministered to the people. As He walked, He healed,
forgave, and taught people. This seemed to be done in the
ordinary schedule of the day.

One more facet stands out for me in today's
scripture—guidance. Only the shepherd can direct our
paths safely. He walked with sure steps along the sandy
shores of Galilee, the lanes of Nazareth, the hills of Judea,
and on the storm-tossed sea. He traveled with steadfast
purpose toward Jerusalem, then climbed the stairs to the
upper room for the last supper with His disciples. He
walked from Gethsemane to Pilate's judgment hall and at
last climbed Calvary's hill, to fulfill, to the *very last detail*,
His Father's will . . . all for us!

*Only one who is thoroughly familiar with the complex,
intricate labyrinth of this world's course is qualified to
be a guide. Lord Jesus, You are the Great Shepherd,
who knows how to care for His sheep. Thank You.*

*But a poor widow came and put in two very small copper
coins, worth only a fraction of a penny. . . . Jesus said,
"I tell you the truth, this poor widow has put more into
the treasury than all the others. . . . she, out of her
poverty, put in everything—all she had to live on."*

—MARK 12:42-44

How much this widow loved You, God! Without
fanfare, without knowing that anyone was watching her
actions, without the praise most of us seek, she gave all
that she had! Here is one of the best examples of integrity
and purity of motive recorded in Your Word.

"She has done what she could," You said of Mary of
Bethany, when she anointed Your feet with the precious oil.
You require no more of us than that, my God . . . but may
I not do less!

It's so easy to do things with our own interest in
mind, to do things because someone is watching, or
because we want to feel better ourselves. Yet our motives,
not outward show, is what You see. You know our hearts
and intentions.

*Please give me a true heart. Help me to forget myself
and do things selflessly. You, Lord, were the selfless one,
sacrificing your life for mine. Help me to be more like You.*

June 9, 1966

Who can snatch the prey from the hands of a mighty man?
Who can demand that a tyrant let his captives go?
But the Lord says, "Even the captives of the most mighty
and most terrible shall all be freed; for I will fight
those who fight you, and I will save your children."

—ISAIAH 49:24-25 TLB

God heard the groaning of the children of Israel who were in Egypt. They were held in cruel slavery by the mighty Pharaoh, and could not free themselves. But God was faithful to the covenant that He made with Abraham, Isaac, and Jacob. With a strong arm He rescued the Israelites, who had been taken captive. The power of Egypt's army was no match for Israel's God.

God hears the groanings of the prisoners today, whether they are in the grip of cruel rulers, in the bondage of sin, or enslaved by grief. For Christians who feel they have failed, sinned beyond forgiveness, or been forsaken by God, there are no more comforting words than these words of Jesus: *They shall never perish, neither shall any man pluck them out of my Father's hand. My Father, which gave them to me is greater than all, and no man is able to pluck them out of my Father's hand. I and My Father are one* (John 10:28-30 KJV).

O God, great is Your faithfulness! Thank you for
rescuing me. Thank You for keeping me. Amen.

 *June 13, 1966*

"For I know the plans I have for you," declares the LORD,
"plans to prosper you and not to harm you, plans to give
you hope and a future. Then you will call upon me and
come and pray to me, and I will listen to you. You will seek
me and find me when you seek me with all your heart."

—JEREMIAH 29:11-13

There is so much that could be written about this
scripture, but my mind centers upon one thought. To find
You, God, and to be found in You, is the whole purpose of
life! To know You is life eternal, and to be in You brings us
our heart's deepest fulfillment. There is no earthly pleasure
or security to compare with the rest, peace, love, and joy
that You alone can give. In Your service is perfect freedom.

I confess to You, my God, that I have not sought You
with all my heart. The delight in riches and the desire for
other things enters my heart, chokes the word, and it
becomes unfruitful.

*But I thank You, Lord, that even through my dullness of
heart and mind, Your light still shines, to reveal the very
things in me which I deplore. Without Your grace, I could
not even know what I am like! Thank You, Lord. Amen.*

June 20, 1966

For everyone looks out for his own interests,
not those of Jesus Christ.

—PHILIPPIANS 2:21

In many subtle ways these words are true of me, O God! There is so much of my life that I live strictly for my own interests—even in the smallest things, Lord.

How quickly I rush to the defense of my own interests.

How easily my routines take precedence over Your purposes.

How quick I am to defend my failures.

How slowly I respond to, and acknowledge, the justice of Your correction.

How timid and self-conscious I am in my attempts to speak to others about You.

How often I fail to make intercession for others after You have "nudged" me by Your Spirit.

How casually I ignore the silent suffering of those around me.

I know that there are so many more I could list. Please bring them to mind, Lord, as I go about my day.

Dear God, thank You that You don't respond to
Your children in such a manner, that You care for us.
Please give me eyes that see, ears that hear, feet
that walk Your path and a heart to do Your will.

June 22, 1966

> *For there stood by me this night the angel of God, whose I am, and whom I serve.*
>
> —ACTS 27:23 KJV

In this incident, recorded in Acts, the Apostle Paul was able to remain calm in the midst of the storm because he knew the one to whom he belonged. His identification had been firmly established long before the crisis. There were no divided loyalties or interests in Paul's life.

It is difficult, if not impossible, to serve effectively in any capacity, if we do not have a heart-interest in what we are doing. Sooner or later, there must come a time in one's life when the decision has to be made for or against God. We cannot remain neutral. Eventually our choices bring us to a "point of no return," not because God wills it so, but because we have chosen it.

Sometimes the revelation comes through our *reactions* to a situation, rather than through our actions. But we will discover, almost without exception, that our path began to diverge away from God through a series of small, seemingly innocent compromises. The wonder of it is that God's unfathomable love and grace reaches out to us, again and again, to draw us back to Him.

> *Dear Lord, let me have no divided interests. I want You to be my only master.*

that our sin is special and cannot be covered by the blood of Christ. It is possible to spend years in vain regrets and sorrow over past mistakes.

Then, there are those who grieve over lost opportunities, sometimes due to circumstances beyond their control. These need to be encouraged to know, and accept the truth, that each moment . . . each day . . . can be a new beginning with God.

Loving Father, You have made every provision for Your people to be fulfilled and productive. We believe in Your great love, forgiveness, and power, which renew us each day.

 *June 27, 1966*

The earth is the Lord's, and everything in it.
—1 CORINTHIANS 10:26

Today I rode the bus from Oklahoma to Marble Falls, Texas, where I am to speak at a church retreat. As I rode, the vastness of Texas, as always, impressed me. God is lavish in His provisions, and Texas reminds me of the magnitude of God. One wonders why we ever doubt Him. The cattle, indeed, on a thousand hills are His. He knows every blade of grass and each brilliant wildflower growing by the roadside.

At dusk, I stepped off the bus at a lonely stop, into the arms of a dear daughter, her husband, and two pairs of childish arms! They were vacationing in the area, and waited here to surprise me. I felt the lavish outpouring of my Father's love and care through the love of my family. He is everywhere present . . . if only we have eyes to see!

> *Lord, You show Your love to us in so many ways*
> *each day . . . through family and friends, through a*
> *stranger's kindness, through the beauty of the simple*
> *wildflower, a tiny part of your creation for us.*
> *I praise You, O God, for all manifestations of*
> *Your bountiful love to me. Amen.*

July 1, 1966

SAN ANTONIO, TEXAS

*Let us fix our eyes on Jesus, the author and perfecter of our
faith, who for the joy set before him endured the cross.*

—HEBREWS 12:2

It has been suggested that, even amidst the
unfathomable agony of the cross, You focused your mind
on "the joy set before you." While I can't know for
certain, I imagine you knew that Satan's power over
mankind would soon be broken, that You would return to
Your Father and the glory which You shared with Him
before the foundation of the world. You knew that fifty
days later, on the day of Pentecost, You, along with the
Father, would send the blessed Holy Spirit, the Spirit of
truth, who would be our guide and comforter forever.

It is satisfying and comforting to remember that You
said that when the Holy Spirit comes, He brings to our
remembrance all things concerning You. This tells me that
I can depend upon the authenticity of the Scriptures. The
truths contained within the pages of Your Word were given
to holy men of God by the revelation of Your Holy Spirit.

*Thank You, Father, for the assurance You give me
that I can accept Your Word as truth. Help me,
when I face difficulties, to look beyond this world
and to set future "joy" in my sight. Amen.*

July 5, 1966

SAN ANTONIO, TEXAS

"Therefore I tell you, do not worry about your life, what you will eat or drink; or about your body, what you will wear. Is not life more important than food, and the body more important than clothes? Therefore do not worry about tomorrow, for tomorrow will worry about itself."

—MATTHEW 6:25,34

I am enjoying my visit with my daughter Kathy and her family. I talk to Paul each day and miss him very much. It has been a long time since I have been away from him for this length of time.

Paul believes God is telling him that our work in Oklahoma is drawing to a close. We do not understand why, but we are beginning to look ahead, to wonder what God has planned for us. We have no idea. He is giving us the privilege of trusting Him, and experiencing a deeper "walk" than we have known. Like Peter, it is tempting to look at the waves . . . to feel apprehension . . . and worry. But Jesus says to us, *Take no thought for the morrow,* and as He said to Peter in the midst of the storm, *Be of good cheer; it is I; be not afraid.*

You, Lord, are the Master of the wind and the waves. Please help me to remember to take a deep breath and know that You are in control of my life.

July 6, 1966

He speaks to the sun and it does not shine; he seals off the light of the stars. He alone stretches out the heavens and treads on the waves of the sea. He is the Maker of the Bear and Orion, the Pleiades and the constellations of the south. He performs wonders that cannot be fathomed, miracles that cannot be counted.

—JOB 9:7-10

Last night, on a hill overlooking the city, we watched a display of fireworks, many miles away. We were on a ranch, visiting friends. From our vantage point, the fireworks appeared as candles, shooting high into the cathedral of darkness. Overhead was the canopy of the stars, whose majesty and glory exceeded the feeble attempts man was making in the distant city. We were enthralled . . . captivated . . . by the same mysteries that caused Job to praise the excellence of his Creator.

It was through Job that God questioned all the generations to come:

Can you bind the chains of the Pleiades, or loose the cords of Orion? Can you lead forth the Mazzaroth in their season, or can you guide the Bear with its children? Do you know the ordinances of the heavens? Can you establish their rule on the earth? (Job 38:31-33 RSV).

What can we answer You, God? What can we say except to proclaim, "My God! How great Thou art!"

43

July 7, 1966

SAN ANTONIO, TEXAS

By faith Abraham, when called to go to a place he would later receive as his inheritance, obeyed and went, even though he did not know where he was going.

—HEBREWS 11:8

Is this Your will for us also, Lord? Are we being given the assignment of walking, as you did, with no "certain resting place?" It is frightening even to contemplate. And yet . . . there can be no greater challenge than the privilege of walking with You in faith.

Without You, Lord, we cannot walk such a road. Even with You, we may falter and fall. You know us far better than we know ourselves. You know our weaknesses and our strengths . . . and whether we are capable of that kind of faith. You also know our desire to serve You and to glorify You through our lives.

We know that You will direct us—every decision, every step. Please help us to walk without worry or fear. The only thing we know for sure is that we are Yours, Lord. What a wonderful security that is!

Trust in the LORD with all your heart and lean not on your own understanding; in all your ways acknowledge him, and he will make your paths straight (Proverbs 3:5,6).

Teach us how to trust You completely.

July 11, 1966

DAVIS, OKLAHOMA

*For since the creation of the world God's invisible
qualities—his eternal power and divine nature—have
been clearly seen, being understood from what
has been made, so that men are without excuse.*

—ROMANS 1:20

I am home again with my beloved after two weeks
absence. It is wonderful to be back in the warmth of Paul's
arms and to have Kathy and the children with us.

As I have meditated on this scripture today, I have
been thinking about family relationships and how
important they are. Through them God's divine order can
be seen and learned. God, in His infinite wisdom, did not
send us into the world to be alone, but placed us together
in families, so that through them He might teach us about
Himself and the greater family of God.

Sometimes barriers exist between family members.
Misunderstandings arise, and the pressures and problems
of life alienate family members from each other. As we
mature, we see how important these relationships are and,
as much as it is in our power, we want to make them right.

*I thank You, Father, for my earthly family, and also
for the spiritual family of which we are a part. Help me
to be sensitive to the needs of my family . . . to realize
each person's value and to do all things in love.*

 *July 12, 1966*

May the Lord make your love increase and
overflow for each other and for everyone else,
just as ours does for you.

—1 Thessalonians 3:12

Increase in love! This should always be our goal. For this is the method ordained of God for us to grow in holiness. I often find myself pleading for more purity. God replies, "Increase in love." In despair at such a demand I cry, "Lord, how hard my growing is!" For this, indeed, is the way of the Cross.

Sometimes it is easier to love those we don't know, than to love those close at hand. Often, we use those who are closest to us to unleash our frustrations and anger. Our Lord loved both, but His dying prayer was for those who were putting Him to death. No better test of our discipleship can be made than loving and interceding for those in our lives who drive the nails! Yet we must also love those who are close—family and friends—and be aware of our actions toward them. Familiarity often blinds us to the deepest needs and hurts of those closest to us.

Loving, forgiving Lord . . . please give me
eyes to see and a heart of love. Amen.

July 18, 1966

Fear of man will prove to be a snare, but whoever trusts in the Lord is kept safe.

—PROVERBS 29:25

Great pressures should remind us that our only responsibility, and our only protection, is to abide in Christ. Today I was confronted with a difficult situation. Paul has not felt well lately, and today he has been in bed. I found it necessary, for his well-being, to make a difficult decision on his behalf. I have a tendency to evade confrontations, and to meet one head-on is an agonizing ordeal for me. My nature is such that I do not like to "make waves." In this instance, my actions may have appeared unkind. However, in my obedience to God's guidance, I became aware that a basic flaw in my character had been overcome today through the power of Christ.

I learned from my physical therapist that it is healthy and encouraging to look back and see progress. In the spiritual realm this is not pride, but the very essence of humility and gratitude, for it honors God. A few years ago I would have been incapable of handling this situation. I would have silently endured it, or fled in anger and frustration. Neither would have been God's way. Today His grace enabled me to do the difficult—but the right—thing.

Thank You, Father, for growth.

 *July 19, 1966*

How priceless is your unfailing love!
Both high and low among men find refuge
in the shadow of your wings.

—PSALM 36:7

Father, we are unsure of our future. My tendency is to become nervous and scared of what lies ahead, to feel a lack of control in not having future circumstances wrapped up neatly. Yet, when we look to You and relinquish our human fears, we are delivered from oppression, fear, and anxiety.

Paul has the growing awareness that You are calling us from this pastorate. Pressures mount because of the uncertainty, but underneath us are Your everlasting arms. There is a fear that we may miss Your guidance, yet You have promised to give us Your wisdom when we need it.

Help us, dear Lord, never to doubt Your love or concern
for us. Paul and I know with our minds that it is better
to walk with You through darkness, than to walk alone
in light. Help us know this with our hearts. As we
face the unknown, grant us the joy of Your presence.
Thank you that You cover us under the shadow
of your powerful wings. Amen.

July 20, 1966

*Give us aid against the enemy, for the help of man
is worthless. With God we will gain the victory,
and he will trample down our enemies.*

—PSALM 108:12-13

In this passage of scripture, I understand the "enemies" as being fear of the future, apprehension, uncertainty, and insecurity. Concluding a pastorate is a lonely experience. There is no one to whom one can actually confide. Even if we could afford that human consolation, it would be a vain comfort, for only God has the answer. Familiar doors are closing and we face the unknown.

It is not the first time we have experienced this. Paul left the business world because he heard God's call to a life of total service. Now he is hearing that call again. At such times as this, one can better understand the isolation Jesus experienced during His last days on Earth. At this time He seems to draw nearer and walks with us in communion and fellowship.

What was it like for You, Jesus, when You began to hear the call to go to Jerusalem? Centuries before it happened, the Psalmist caught Your thoughts: *Then I said, "Here I am, I have come—it is written about me in the scroll. I desire to do your will, O my God; your law is within my heart"* (Psalm 40:7,8).

*Help us, Lord, to desire Your will,
no matter where it takes us. Amen.*

July 24, 1966

Behold, I will create new heavens and a new earth.
The former things will not be remembered,
nor will they come to mind.

—Isaiah 65:17

I took Paul to the Dallas airport today. He is going to San Francisco to meet a group of Christian Church leaders who are interested in starting a new congregation.

God is always doing new things, and as this scripture indicates, He is preparing a "new" world for Paul and me . . . where, we do not know. It is becoming easier now to live by faith . . . one day at a time. The tomorrows do not seem so important . . . it is the *now* which counts.

How we minister to the needs of our congregation at this time is of greater value than anticipating the future. We must give Christ's love to these people in spite of our own uncertainties. Some of them do not understand. We are meeting some opposition over our decision to leave. We have had a wonderful ministry here, and for the first time we are experiencing some problems and frustrations. Some are grieved and simply do not want us to leave. Others cannot understand how Paul knows God is telling him to leave.

Even in this we can praise You, O God.
What we are experiencing can mean a deepening
companionship with You! The greater the need,
the greater Your grace. For this we thank You.

July 28, 1966

To every thing there is a season and a time to every purpose under heaven . . . a time to laugh . . . a time to embrace . . . to get . . . to keep . . . a time to love.

—ECCLESIASTES 3:1-8 KJV

There are moments in one's life which are so precious that they must be held lightly, so fragile are they . . . so uniquely special and God-given. Their unearthly beauty could be shattered by too heavy a touch.

This day has contained such moments. Here in a Dallas motel, Kathy and her children are waiting with me for Paul's return tomorrow from California. It is a special time of togetherness only God could have planned. These golden hours are like beautiful gems in the long rosary of one's life. The children played and splashed in the swimming pool as Kathy and I talked, and occasionally went into the water to be with them. Overhead was the cloudless blue of a Texas sky. These are moments of intimate fellowship recorded in my memory forever— mother and daughter, grandmother and grandchildren. I am blessed.

Thank you, Father, for these memorable hours with my loved ones. How blessed I am to have them in my life. Because of Your Presence, we are experiencing a touch of heaven!

July 29, 1966

DALLAS, TEXAS

For we walk not by faith, not by sight.

—2 CORINTHIANS 5:7 KJV

It is 5:00 A.M. and I am writing in my journal as I wait for Paul's plane to arrive from San Francisco. I feel very alone at this early hour . . . an island set apart from all these other human islands. Each person is wrapped in his or her own private thoughts. Yet the quiet early morning lends to a feeling of time standing still. There are sleepy families, service men, flight attendants, pilots, and workmen in overalls. Back at the motel, Kathy and the children are sleeping.

So much is hanging in the balance at this moment. What is Paul's decision? Are we to resign the Davis pastorate? When? Are we accepting a call from California? Only God knows.

Paul's plane is now landing.

O Father! You know I don't want to move so far away! Help me pray "Thy Will . . . not mine . . . be done." Help me to desire Your will above all else . . . more than my own. For it is in obedience to Your will that the true riches of life are found. I offer You my praise before I know what our decision will be. Thank You, Father, for this grace. Amen.

August 1, 1966

*Pray for us that the message of the Lord may spread
rapidly and be honored, just as it was with you.*

—2 THESSALONIANS 3:1

Yesterday morning, after the worship service, Paul
submitted his resignation, giving two months' notice. He
has not arrived at a definite decision in respect to the
work in California. He still has the conviction, however,
that God is saying time is drawing near for our departure
from the Davis church. The decision took great courage
and faith on his part, for we face an unknown future.
Paul's commitment to his Lord is so total, that there is
never any wavering in his obedience, once he is confident
of God's leading.

In many respects it was a glorious service, although a
difficult one for Paul. He came back from California tired
and physically drained. His recurring weariness concerns
me. However, God's love flowing to us through our
congregation was healing and beautiful. What a special
part of Christ's body is this wonderful group of people!

*Help us all, Father, as we make this transition. Give Paul an
extra measure of strength. Please show us where you want us
to go. Thank you that we can rest easy in Your divine care.*

August 2, 1966

The fear of the LORD is the beginning of knowledge, but fools despise wisdom and discipline.

—PROVERBS 1:7

The fear of God, as used in this passage of scripture, is not referring to the negative emotions we ordinarily associate with fear. It does not mean dread, terror, or apprehension. Rather, it has to do with awe, respect, reverence. The fear of God must precede any real knowledge of Him. Our human tendency is to form our own image of God.

This is why knowledge of God's word is of paramount importance. God has given us His Word so that we may come to know Him as *He desires to be known.* He wants us to know His character and attributes, so that we may have fellowship with Him. The key to knowing God through His Word is to approach it with openness and humility.

And so we know and rely on the love God has for us. God is love. Whoever lives in love lives in God, and God in him. In this way, love is made complete among us so that we will have confidence on the day of judgment, because in this world we are like him. There is no fear in love. But perfect love drives out fear, because fear has to do with punishment. The one who fears is not made perfect in love (1 John 4:16-18).

**God, help me to fear You, in reverence and awe,
and not to fear the circumstances of life.**

August 4, 1966

He brought them forth with silver and gold; and there was not one feeble person among their tribes.

—PSALM 105:37 KJV

O God! Great is Your faithfulness! You not only led Your people out of slavery but You also caused the Egyptians to strip themselves of their jewelry and give it to their Hebrew slaves before they left Egypt on that Passover night. Every material need was met . . . their health was preserved, and even the aged had their "youth renewed as the eagles." How You loved and cared for Your people.

Can we trust You to do as much for us? Indeed, we want to trust You to do that very thing. Our age is nothing to You. Our poverty will be met by Your riches and our health will be preserved until the work to which You call us is completed.

My Father answers through His Word:

But I will not take my love from him, nor will I ever betray my faithfulness. I will not violate my covenant or alter what my lips have uttered (Psalm 89:33-34).

I offer You my song of praise tonight, Lord . . . for no other reason except that I love You!

Jesus himself came up and walked along with them.

—LUKE 24:15

The two disciples were despairing and hopeless that day, as they walked on the road to Emmaus. They had just witnessed the crucifixion of their Lord, and the light had gone out of their world. But, as they walked along, sorrowfully discussing these events, Jesus Himself drew near and began walking with them. What an experience! How their hearts must have thrilled, in retrospect, as they remembered those marvelous moments when their risen Savior had walked with them, and taught from scriptures the things which had been written of Him.

At first, they did not recognize Him. They were conscious only of their sorrow and loss. While He sat at the table with them, breaking bread, their eyes were opened, and they were able to see the Lord Jesus Christ in His resurrection life.

So it is with us. We become absorbed in our sorrows and problems, and it is only as we spend time in God's presence that our spiritual eyes are opened to see Him. He is always with us, but we have myopic vision and do not recognize Him.

O God, my Savior! To spend time with You each day is the way I too shall come to see You. Grant me the grace of clearer vision, Lord, that I may see You.

August 11, 1966

*If any of you lacks wisdom, he should ask God,
who gives generously to all without finding fault.*

—JAMES 1:5

Paul and I are feeling so unsure about our future,
Lord, what we should do and where we should go. It gives
me great comfort to know that You always honor Your
Word! This scripture in James indicates that You do not
want Your children to remain uncertain. You assure us You
desire to give us Your wisdom in times of decision making.

At this point in our lives we cannot possibly know
which decisions we need to make. Do we stay here awhile
and minister to these precious people? There are some new
Christians who need to be nurtured, Lord. Or, do we leave
now? We are willing to do either. Show us, in some specific
way, Your will for us and give us grace to follow in
obedience. I thank You now, Lord, for Your answer.

*So do not fear for I am with you. Do not be
dismayed, for I am your God. I will strengthen you and
help you; I will uphold you with my righteous right hand*
(Isaiah 41:10).

Thank you, my God, for your amazing words of comfort.

August 18, 1966

1:30 A.M.

Let the beloved of the LORD rest secure in him,
for he shields him all day long, and the one
the LORD loves rests between his shoulders.

—DEUTERONOMY 33:12

Have I not commanded you? Be strong and courageous.
Do not be terrified; do not be discouraged, for the
LORD your God will be with you wherever you go.

—JOSHUA 1:9

My sheep listen to my voice; I know them, and they
follow me. I give them eternal life, and they shall never
perish; no one can snatch them out of my hand.

—JOHN 10:27-28

See, I have engraved you on the palms of my hands.

—ISAIAH 49:16

In the depths and heart of God's love, His people lie
secure. Unable to sleep tonight, these scriptures bring me a
sense of security, comfort, and peace. It is in the arms of
God that the weary and anxious child, like a wounded
bird, may find rest.

Even the sparrow has found a home, and the swallow a nest
for herself, where she may have her young—a place near
your altar, O Lord Almighty, my King and my God.

—PSALM 84:3

I give You praise, wonderful, wonderful God!

August 21, 1966

And you will be my witnesses in Jerusalem, and in all Judea and Samaria, and to the ends of the earth.

—ACTS 1:8

This morning a letter arrived from a member of the congregation Paul met with in California. The letter was a plea for us to come, an expression of a personal longing for a deeper walk with God in as honest and graphic a way as I have ever seen it expressed. It was a beautiful letter. I felt my resistance crumbling.

The letter echoed the anguish that once throbbed in my own heart. There was a day when I pulled my car to the side of a highway and wept bitterly . . . in anger and frustration. I had driven a considerable distance to hear the message of a man I believed would bring me inspiration and teaching in Christian growth. Instead . . . I was fed husks.

With my head bowed over the steering wheel, I cried, "O God! Surely there must be more than this!" It was at that point in my life I turned away from the church and its teachings, in a desperate search for the reality of God. I wandered for a number of years in the confusing labyrinth of world religions and philosophies, some of which excluded Jesus Christ. Now I have come full circle, more grounded in my faith and in the church.

O God, from this point on, I withhold nothing from You!

> *Remember how the LORD your God led you all*
> *the way in the desert these forty years, to humble*
> *you and to test you in order to know what was in your*
> *heart . . . He gave you manna to eat in the desert.*

— DEUTERONOMY 8:2,16

Sometimes it is helpful to look back over the years and see how carefully God has watched over us. Even before we were born, the Psalmist informs us in Psalm 119, in our mother's womb, God knew us.

This should be of special comfort to parents who are anxious and distraught about their children. Many parents today suffer anguish and heartbreak when their children rebel and go their own way. The greatest safety we can give our children is to put God first in our own lives, and then surrender them to Him. He cares about them more than we possibly can, and our own relationship with God is their greatest insurance. In times when our sons have been away from us, I have prayed, "Father, I will tell others about Your Son, and trust You to care for mine." He has not failed! Our children come from us, and are loaned to us for a time, to love and nurture, but they belong to God.

> *God, I know that You love our children more*
> *than we ever could, and You will care for them*
> *with tenderness and mercy. Thank You.*

August 25, 1966

At daybreak Jesus went out to a solitary place.
The people were looking for him . . . they tried to keep
him from leaving them. But he said, "I must preach
the good news of the kingdom of God to the other
towns also, because that is why I was sent."

—LUKE 4:42-44

An attempt has been made this week to circulate a petition asking us to remain in Davis. Realizing that Paul would not be swayed by public opinion, it was dropped. While in a local store this week, the woman at the cash register said, "You both have brought the love of Jesus Christ into our community. This is why it is so difficult to see you leave." We realize, and are trying to help them to understand that it is not us they are clinging to, but the One we represent.

Often, when we first arrived in Davis, members of our congregation would follow us home on Sunday nights. Sometimes they left at midnight, or later, reluctant to go home . . . not knowing exactly why. In their words, they felt there was "something different" about us . . . a dimension of love and power that they could not quite understand. There is a difference between a pastor who ministers intellectually to his congregation, and one who has a heart-ministry to his people.

Lord, may we always show that type of love—
Your love—wherever we go.

 *August 28, 1966*

*So David triumphed over the Philistine with a
sling and a stone; without a sword in his hand
he struck down the Philistine and killed him.*

—1 SAMUEL 17:50

We must fight our giants with the weapons God
provides . . . not our own. Our real warfare is not against
individuals, as in the case of David, but against Satan's
strongholds. Only God knows the weapons that can
prevail. In David's case the weapon was not King Saul's
armor, which was offered to him, but a sling and a stone.
Guided by God, the stone struck the one vulnerable spot in
Goliath's armor. David used the weapon he trusted, but it
was God who gave the victory. The Spirit of God guides us
to the right weapon and shows us how to use it.

This is contrary to the rationalism of the world. It is
our human nature to rely on our own senses and reason
when faced with insurmountable circumstances. Self-effort
always has been one of Satan's most appealing snares. He
wins the battle every time he entices us into self-reliance,
rather than looking to God.

*Father, this is a very difficult lesson to learn. But I
praise You that slowly, step by step, I am learning it.
Help me to rely on You more and more each day.*

August 30, 1966

*If you believe, you will receive whatever
you ask for in prayer.*

—MATTHEW 21:22

I awakened this morning with this scripture on my mind. Later, I was to use it . . . not for myself, but for my friends. These days of prayer with Peggy, Faye, Auda, and Hettie, are significant. We have been prayer partners for a long time, and these are our last days together. We are allowing God to use them to strengthen us.

When we met this morning, I felt God wanted me to pray for them in preparation for the days ahead. Encouraged by this scripture, I went to each one and prayed. We felt the blessing of our Lord's wonderful presence in our midst. We needed Him, for we are each being "stretched" these days—being made more than we are. It is painful, but necessary. Stretching is one of God's ways of maturing His people.

Father, grant us the grace to willingly submit to Your stretching. It is when we are increased that more of You may be contained. Let the benediction of Your love rest upon those who remain here, and upon the one who leaves. May each of us, in her own way, and in her own place, be instruments of Your peace. Amen.

For the cloud of the LORD was upon the tabernacle by day, and fire was on it by night, in the sight of all the house of Israel throughout all their journeys.

—EXODUS 40:38 KJV

We spent today packing books and boxes in preparation for our departure. Packing can be a lonely business, especially when one's heart is heavy about leaving a beloved place. We are conscious of the Lord's presence with our congregation and in our lives. I praise God for the comfort of His Holy Spirit; we look to that same Spirit for guidance on our journey.

God leads His people today as He once led the children of Israel by cloud and fire. He has promised that He will never leave us. We are walking in joy and peace because we know our Shepherd is going before us. The weight of this church is being lifted because we have cast our burden upon the Lord and He is sustaining us. We are learning to rejoice in His faithfulness, knowing that God is preparing a place for us "in the wilderness" of the unknown.

Thank You, dear Lord, for giving us the privilege of walking with You by faith, rather than by sight. Amen.

September 7, 1966

*Therefore, I tell you, her many sins
have been forgiven—for she loved much.
But he who has been forgiven little loves little.*

—LUKE 7:47

This scripture portrays an interesting and beautiful aspect of the character of the Lord Jesus Christ. It reveals the simple, innate dignity of the Son of God, in what could have been an embarrassing situation.

Jesus had been invited to the home of Simon, the Pharisee. In that day, it was customary to bathe the feet of the guests as they arrived. It was an act of hospitality and respect. Simon did not perform this courtesy to Jesus when He arrived . . . a flagrant act of disrespect.

Entering the scene was the woman, whom Scripture defines as "an especially wicked woman" (Amplified version). From the moment she arrived, she ceased not to kiss the Lord's feet, bathing them with her tears . . . and this in the presence of some of the city's most distinguished religious leaders! The woman's dramatic act of devotion reveals touching humility and brokenness, which come from genuine repentance. Jesus was neither offended nor embarrassed by her. Rather, He welcomed her with love and joy. Jesus' words to Simon in the above scripture merit our serious reflection.

*God, may my measure of love for You equal
Your great measure of forgiveness toward me.*

September 13, 1966

In the beginning was the Word, and the Word was with God, and the Word was God. He was in the beginning with God: all things were made through Him, and without Him was not anything made that was made.

—JOHN 1:1-3 KJV

These words tell me that You are indeed my God. The wonder and glory of its reality is beyond my comprehension. I see through a glass darkly. It will take all of eternity to be able to bear the full knowledge of Your majesty and love.

You are the pearl of great price, the fairest of ten thousands, altogether lovely! You are the beginning and the end of my faith. I would like to know You as John knew You . . . Your eyes a flame of fire, Your feet as fine brass . . . Your voice as many waters (Revelation 1:14-15). I would like to know You as Peter knew You . . . Great Shepherd of the sheep, Bishop of my soul (1 Peter 2:25). I want to seek You always . . . the one good and perfect, holy and righteous God.

You are all love . . . power . . . wisdom . . . perfection . . . compassion . . . mercy . . . forgiveness . . . my all . . . forever and ever! I praise You for all of the amazing facets of Your character—great and living God.

September 20, 1966

*Enlarge the place of your tent, stretch
your tent curtains wide, do not hold back;
lengthen your cords, strengthen your stakes.*

—ISAIAH 54:2

You are speaking to me through these words, my God. I am conscious of my great need to be stretched and strengthened by You. Otherwise, the strong winds of the unknown will be too much for me. My "stakes" must go down deep into the solid rock of Your faithfulness. I want to be aware of the parts of my life I need to give to You in order to have stakes that hold. Then, as the cords are lengthened, the fresh winds of Your Holy Spirit can blow through the "tent" that I am.

Through the eyes of faith I like to think of that little tent in the strong gales—flapping at times, perhaps, yet holding firm—an invitation to weary, lonely travelers to find shelter. Please show me how to strengthen every cord of my being, that I may stand strong against the storms of life.

Guide those who you wish to "dwell in my tent" and give me the discretion and power to love them as You would, O Lord. And, please, dwell in my tent, O God!

Can a mother forget the baby at her breast and have no compassion on the child she has borne? Though she may forget, I will not forget you! See, I have engraved you on the palms of my hands; your walls are ever before me.

—ISAIAH 49:15-16

In this lovely passage of scripture, God is communicating how tenderly He loves us. Simple but powerful analogies are used to help us understand: a woman with her nursing child; the palm of a hand. Even as our own palms are a familiar and essential part of us; so, God is saying, we are held intimately and closely to His heart. And though a human forsake us—even a mother— He will never forget His people.

How amazing it is that God, in all His power and glory, would remember us. And not only remember us, but love us and send His Son as a sacrifice for our sins.

Lord, when I am rebellious, or simply not thinking of You the way I should, please let me remember Your remembrance of me, your love for me, and for all mankind. For You are full of compassion and tender mercy.

October 1, 1966

I have set the LORD always before me. Because he is at my right hand, I will not be shaken.

—PSALM 16:8

This past Sunday was our last in Davis. The men's chorus, so dear to Paul's heart, sang "Hallelujah, We Shall Rise" and the choir sang "He Is Everything To Me." Paul's text was from Luke 24:28-31 . . . the story of Jesus walking with His disciples on the road to Emmaus on Resurrection Day.

Today's hours flew by on wings. Jack, Kathy, and the children were here with trucks to help us move. Friends and neighbors came to help us load. There were quick good-byes and last glimpses of familiar landmarks as we drove away. We are at a motel in Ardmore tonight and will go on to San Antonio tomorrow. Now it is over . . . and the dear people of Davis are receding and becoming a part of our past . . . and yet . . . held always in our hearts.

Father, there is a lonely space in my heart tonight. This is one of the hardest parts of life—change—and disconnecting from the familiar. From the grocery store and local "scenery" to the people who make up the core of one's life. The feeling of not belonging anywhere is an unusual experience for me. I already miss the friends we are leaving behind.

Lord, I set You before me. Help my faith to stand independent of any situation. I trust You to fill this vacuum with Yourself, and I offer You my praise.

October 3, 1966

But godliness with contentment is great gain.
For we brought nothing into the world, and
we can take nothing out of it.

—1 TIMOTHY 6:6-7

At the beginning of my spiritual journey, the writings of the early saints greatly influenced my thinking. The doctrine of "detachment" from possessions made a deep and lasting impression, and probably helped to prepare me for my present experience. As we unpack and I see my belongings mingling with Kathy's, I have a curious sense of relief. I am being freed from attachment to things, even though there are still some possessions I treasure . . . particularly my beloved books. I have the feeling I am being "stripped for action" and find myself thinking more and more of God and His next "assignment" for us.

It is important to develop balance in respect to possessions. With much of the world in poverty and want, it is good to take stock of what we actually need. The desire for things can become an obsession and subtly take the place of our desire to grow closer to God.

Dear Father, in the days which are ahead, may Paul
and I come to know the truth of these words. Amen.

October 8, 1966

If I take the wings of the morning, and dwell in the uttermost parts of the sea; even there shall thy hand lead me, and thy right hand shall hold me.

—PSALM 139:9-10 KJV

This scripture reminds me that there is no place where God is not. There is no sin so black, no situation so hopeless, no place so inaccessible, that God's love cannot reach. It comforts me to know that even tears shed in the darkness of night are seen by God; because darkness and the light are the same to Him.

Jesus said that even a little sparrow could not fall to the ground without the Father's knowledge. The secret tears and anguish of the most desperate heart in an unreached land find response in God's heart of infinite love . . . and a tiny flower hidden in the most remote mountain pass brings joy to His heart, as it blooms . . . unnoticed by any eye but His.

O God, my Father! I lift my heart in praise to You because of Your knowledge of the most infinitesimal need in Your great universe. I am amazed and can barely comprehend this thought. You are also aware of me.

Share with God's people who are in need.
Practice hospitality.

—ROMANS 12:13

Father, we are grateful for the hospitality and love we have found in this home with our children. It has been opened to us graciously. There has been a certain degree of inconvenience and confusion, as is natural when a household has more people, more furniture and possessions. However, it is not the fact that this home has been opened to us that is so wonderful; but the grace with which it has been done.

Grant, O God, that we may receive with equal grace! We are playing a new role these days . . . one of dependency upon others. During most of our lives, our role has been to serve, to give, to open our home to others, to share materially with those in need. You know, Father, this type of lifestyle has been my dread; to be dependent in any way upon others has been abhorrent to me.

Now . . . here I am . . . Lord, being and doing that which I most dreaded! May Your grace be sufficient for us, and Your blessing rest richly upon this lovely home and the wonderful people who have accepted us with such unreserved grace.

October 14, 1966

*And for this we labor and strive, that we have put
our hope in the living God, who is the Savior of
all men, and especially of those who believe.*

—1 TIMOTHY 4:10

Within a few days, in all probability, we will be leaving
for California. This will be a trip to ascertain whether we
both feel God is leading us there in service.

Some find it difficult to understand why we are taking
such a confident step into an uncertain future. How can
others understand that we are simply following Jesus, as
we believe He is leading us? To some it seems foolish—to
us, natural and right. We believe we see, down this
unknown road of the future, individuals waiting who are
in need of Christ and His love.

To the outside world we must appear as a foolish
married couple, with graying hair and a good portion of
our lives behind us, heading out into the unknown—
without home, bed, or income. What they cannot see are
two hearts beating in unison and love for our Lord and
each other. They cannot see the joy and expectancy in our
hearts at this high privilege that is ours.

> *Guide us, God, as we step out, only by
> faith in Your great love and guidance.*

October 18, 1966

HOLBROOK, ARIZONA

You turned my wailing into dancing; you removed my sackcloth and clothed me with joy, that my heart may sing to you and not be silent. O LORD my God, I will give you thanks forever.

—PSALM 30:11-12

It was difficult leaving our family yesterday morning. As Paul and I traveled westward, I reflected on the above scripture and realized once more that there is no sacrifice I can make which could ever repay what God has done for me.

Today we drove across New Mexico, through mountain passes and stark desert beauty . . . mile after mile of emptiness . . . too vast to comprehend. Endless miles of telephone poles stretched away in the distance, as far as the eye could see.

As we drove, my mind was occupied with thoughts of those who risk everything for Christ . . . living out their lives in lonely, far away places. Their love for Him is so intense because they actually *know* Christ—not merely *about* Him. Those who are willing to risk little for Christ, whose faith is shallow, do not really know Him . . . no matter how loud their profession. For to know Him as He is means to love Him supremely. I am not there yet . . . but I know that knowledge and love go hand in hand. They are two sides of the same coin.

Lord, give me the will and the wisdom to truly love You more.

October 20, 1966

LEE VINING, CALIFORNIA

*O Lord, when you favored me, you made my mountain
stand firm; but when you hid your face, I was dismayed.*

—PSALM 30:7

Today we drove through rugged mountain passes,
down lonely canyons and across desert floors of swirling
dust into California. These mountains had no foliage to
relieve their monotony, but were stark and naked against
the sky. At times the wind howled around us, and on the
distant High Sierras, we could see the blowing snow, like
powdery dust. When we broke through the mountain pass
at last, it was to descend into a lovely sunlit valley.

As the miles rolled behind us, today's scripture was
brought home to me in a personal way.

*Lord, by Your favor, You have made my mountain
stand strong. The long, seemingly endless highway,
stretching across the lonely desert, reminded me of a bleak
period in my life. I was once like those shifting, desert
sands . . . unstable, confused. Sometimes I was as desolate
as the desert over which I was traveling. But You God, my
Father, gathered the sands of my life, and made them into
a mountain . . . a mountain of praise to You.*

**God, You alone could gather the fragmented person I was and
make me whole. There is no limit to Your love and grace!**

October 21, 1966

Let us hold unswervingly to the hope we profess,
for he who promised is faithful.

—HEBREWS 10:23

Today we have arrived at our destination and are spending tonight with new friends.

I am remembering a lesson God taught me on our trip. As we traveled across the desert, we sometimes saw, miles ahead of us, the hazy outline of another mountain. It would appear to us as impassable, and as we approached, we would speculate—will the road go over the mountain, around it, or tunnel through?

When we got close, we were invariably astounded at the very simple, natural way road engineers had solved the problem. They obviously knew their business and we would proceed, confident that the unknown road would lead us safely through the pass. Once on the other side of the mountain, there would open before us new, unimagined vistas of beauty. It made the rugged, sometimes arduous, climb extraordinarily worthwhile! However, without the inner vision and hope, we would have had no joy on the journey itself, and the climb would have been far more tedious. God's people must retain God's vision.

Dear Lord, You are teaching me, day by day, to praise You by
faith, so tonight I offer You once more my sacrifice of praise.
Let my prayer be set forth before You as incense, and the
lifting up of my hands as the evening sacrifice. Amen.

October 24, 1966

For where your treasure is, there your heart will be also.
—MATTHEW 6:21

Today Paul and I moved into a small apartment. Perhaps by having a place of our own I will be able to find God and recover from this desperate homesickness. I will have more time to pray and read my Bible.

While thinking about the above scripture, I must ask myself: Where is my treasure? Detachment, I am discovering, is not so easy after all! In spite of inward pain, however, today my will is becoming more centered on God's purposes. I am beginning to focus with my heart and I am getting God's perspective.

Dear Father, forgive my weakness! Help me to be identified with Your will and to lose myself in Your love. You know me so well. You have always known that people— the ones I love—are where I am most vulnerable. This is my Achilles' heel. I feel lost when I am living away from the people whom I love and who love me—friends, family.

I know this gives me the opportunity to know You better my great Father, to look to You for all my needs. I am leaning hard upon You tonight, Lord.

 *October 26, 1966*

*Though the fig tree does not bud and there are no
grapes on the vines, though the olive crop fails
and the fields produce no food, though there are
no sheep in the pen and no cattle in the stalls,
yet I will rejoice in the LORD.*

—HABAKKUK 3:17-19

This wonderful scripture was sent to me today by my friend, Peggy. It tells me that we do not have to have everything going our way to have joy in the Lord. If He is indeed the Lord of our lives, then our real joy and peace, as well as our strength, will come from Him.

How difficult it is to separate ourselves from our circumstances, our emotions, our humanity. How easy it is to dwell on how we feel, and judge our circumstances using that measure. Yet God promises us: *They that wait upon the Lord shall renew their strength, they shall mount up with wings as eagles; they shall run and not be weary; and they shall walk and not faint* (Isaiah 40:31 KJV). His Spirit can supercede our human condition.

***Please help me to focus on You.
Help Paul and I to wait upon You, Lord.***

November 2, 1966

For the LORD searches every heart and
understands every motive behind the thoughts.
If you seek him, he will be found by you.

—1 CHRONICLES 28:9

I am very grateful, Lord, that You know me exactly as I am. This is comfort and security for me. I cannot fool You, nor hide any area of my life from Your eyes.

You, O God—Who knows the heart and its every dream and imagination—can never be satisfied with giving us less than Your highest, for You are all love. This is why it is so important for us to make a total surrender of our lives to You. You have nothing but our good in mind when You bring us to Yourself. You have promised that You will bring us to our "desired haven" (Psalm 107:30).

Often we do not know our real desire when we begin our life with You, but You know; and as we are able to comprehend, it is slowly revealed to us. The latter part of today's scripture defines it clearly: it is YOU!

I praise You, my Lord, for the assurance You give me that I may find You and know You. This is all my desire—to know You.

November 3, 1966

You, O LORD, keep my lamp burning;
my God turns my darkness into light.

—PSALM 18:28

Today a letter came from our friend, David DePlessis, telling of a Christian meeting to be held tomorrow at Stockton—so close to us! David wrote us airmail from Washington, D.C., and it reached us in time! We have felt a need for spiritual fellowship since we have been here. Now the Lord has opened this door for us.

Sometimes we think we are walking all alone, but if God knows we need other Christians to encourage us, He will send them to us. What an amazing bond we have as brothers and sisters in Christ. The Psalmist wrote: *The LORD makes darkness His secret place* (Psalm 18:11 KJV) and God promises: *And I will give you the treasures of darkness and hidden riches of secret places* (Isaiah 45:3 KJV). God knows exactly how to probe the darkness and bring forth the deep hidden treasures, which are for our delight.

Blessed are You, Lord! Guardian and savior of my soul.

November 7, 1966

If the LORD delights in a man's way, he makes
his steps firm; though he stumble, he will not fall,
for the LORD upholds him with his hand.

—PSALM 37:23,24

Yesterday, the Lord suddenly lifted the veil from our mountain and revealed the shining pathway of His present will for us. We received—and accepted—His call to help the people establish a church here in Antioch for His glory. The call from the congregation came without one dissenting vote.

Last night during the worship service, I had a feeling of great joy, for these people had suddenly become *my* people . . . their joy, sorrow, and problems were now mine. The Lord, by His Spirit, had placed us in this part of His body, and I was identified with them—*not by might, nor by power, but by My Spirit, says the LORD Almighty* (Zechariah 4:6).

I have made an amazing discovery! When our wills are fully yielded to Him, His will becomes our delight! Our Lord, speaking through the Psalmist, said; *I desire to do your will, O my God; your law is within my heart* (Psalm 40:8).

Father, let Your will always be done in me.
May it become, increasingly, my delight. Amen.

November 14, 1966

May the LORD keep watch between you and me
when we are away from each other.

—GENESIS 31:49

We are on the road again to visit our beloved family for the holidays! This morning we said good-bye to Al and Elaine and the community, which only a short time ago meant nothing to us. Now it has come within the orbit of our concern. Its people are important to us.

The apartment in which we lived, the streets we walked, the places we shopped, the mountains, the rivers . . . all are firmly established in our hearts. We have worshipped here; had fellowship with a special community of God's people; and also experienced the pain and the joy of new surrender to God's will. And we have left behind a part of ourselves.

I am ever amazed at the flux of life and how close we can become to people in such a short time.

God, I ask Your blessing on these people. Help me
always to be aware and ready to meet the people You would
have me meet, to be able to show them Christ, living in me.
Prepare the way for Paul and I when we return.

November 17, 1966

TUCSON, ARIZONA

*In this way, love is made complete among us so that we will
have confidence on the day of judgement, because in this
world we are like him. There is no fear in love.*

—1 JOHN 4:17,18

Tonight we are staying with Paul's sister-in-law, Ruth.
Paul has been in considerable pain today and drove with
his coat thrown over his right shoulder. We concluded the
air-conditioner might be too cold for him, but the weather
was too warm to drive without it. He has gone to bed, and
I sit alone, writing in my journal.

I am thinking tonight of what it actually means to
have friendship with Jesus. It will be of eternal importance
on that great day of meeting! Scripture tells me that if
Jesus and I become good friends here, I will not cringe in
fear and guilt when I meet Him face to face, nor will I
shrink from His clear-eyed appraisal. My sins will all be at
the Cross, cleansed by His Blood.

When we meet, there will be joyful, mutual
recognition by two who already know and love one
another. John also tells us that as Christ is, so are we in
this world. In other words, we share the same nature.
Amazing grace! I am a "stranger and pilgrim" in this
world, but there I will be a citizen. I will have come home!

*Dearest Lord, Jesus, it is impossible for me to fear one I love.
When You call me finally to Yourself, it is my prayer that I
may come to You with my love "made perfect." Amen.*

November 20, 1966

*Stand fast therefore in the liberty wherewith
Christ hath made us free, and be not entangled
again with the yoke of bondage.*

—GALATIANS 5:1 KJV

We are "home" again with our family.

Reading God's Word tonight in the quietness of our room, I came to this passage of scripture. It kindles my heart into flames of joy and praise . . . releasing a song and a prayer. A song as I remember my Savior's hand striking the fetters which set me free, and a prayer that I shall never again be in bondage to anything or anyone but the Lord Jesus Christ.

O God . . . my Savior . . . Liberator . . . Redeemer . . . Lord! I love to praise Your name. Bound to You with cords of love, I have found perfect freedom. When pressure and anxiety come, I flee to You, and I find peace. It is there I commune with You, and find a song. The Spirit is singing within my soul. Although I am held captive in human flesh . . . my spirit soars when I think of Your greatness and love! Purest of all . . . most holy . . . all love . . . Jesus. *You are to give him the name Jesus, because he will save his people from their sins* (Matthew 1:21).

*It is my delight to walk with You, and my desire,
O God, to love You more and more. I trust You to
enable me to love You increasingly, and to perfect all
which concerns me—forever and ever. Amen.*

November 22, 1966

But the Counselor, the Holy Spirit, whom the Father will send in my name, will teach you all things and will remind you of everything I have said to you.

—JOHN 14:26

Paul and I are alone tonight in the "piney woods" of east Texas. The retreat starts tomorrow, and we have the lodge to ourselves. A lovely room has been assigned to us. Outside there is a beautiful full moon, and an illuminated cross casts its reflection on the quiet lake beneath our window. We have traveled many miles . . . from "Antioch" to "Palestine" . . . and now it is wonderful to be here; to rest in each other's arms—and in God's. How we cherish such times of peace and quietness.

We both pray that God, by His Spirit, will find in us clean, open channels through which He can pour His truth and love.

Let me, my God, hold on to Your truth carefully and in purity. I pray that You will empty me of "self," and allow the Spirit to teach me—and teach through me—that others may see Your power, love, and truth. Thank You for the words of the above verse, what assurance they are to me. Thank You for remaining with us. Amen.

November 26, 1966

> *But grow in the grace and knowledge of*
> *our Lord and Savior Jesus Christ. To him*
> *be glory both now and forever! Amen.*

—2 PETER 3:18

The retreat ended at noon today. It brought everyone many blessings from God, expressed through one another.

Paul has been extremely tired and spent much of his time resting in our room. Friends here have prayed for him, and this morning he felt strong enough to give the morning meditation in the chapel. He conducted the beautiful, early morning Communion service, and shared with us a recent experience:

Kneeling at the Communion table, early one morning in our church, the sacred elements suddenly became vibrant with life as he held them in his hands. He spoke on a more powerful level than I have ever heard him speak, on the reality of a living Savior.

God permitted us not only to minister, but to be ministered to by many loving friends. I have been asked to return next year to be a co-leader with another of God's servants.

I kneel at Your feet, my Savior, to give You thanks.
It was a joy to speak for You, and let You bring forth through
me the truths which could bless and feed Your people.

November 28, 1966

ATHENS, TEXAS

Let your eyes look straight ahead, fix your gaze directly before you. Make level paths for your feet and take only ways that are firm. Do not swerve to the right or the left; keep your foot from evil.

—PROVERBS 4:25-27

We have lingered an extra day in east Texas, to visit with our friends the Woodruffs, and with Grady and Peggy Kennedy, who drove from Oklahoma to be with us.

It is easy and a great temptation to have lingering thoughts and want to return to former joys and accomplishments, or to have anxious forebodings of the future. In the above scripture, God tells us our attention and energies are to be focused on the present. We are instructed to keep our eyes on our goal, not to the right or the left, forward or behind.

In this way we shall neither be inflated by former victories nor depressed by past failures. We need not be apprehensive for the future. We cannot improve upon God's wisdom! He knows exactly the teaching needed to keep us safe and in peace. Jesus also instructs us in the words: *Do not worry about tomorrow, for tomorrow will worry about itself. Each day has enough trouble of its own* (Matthew 6:34).

> *Father dear, I have a nagging concern for Paul these days. Please help me not to look ahead and to trust You with my dearest possession. Amen.*

 *December 2, 1966*

The king is enthralled by your beauty; honor him, for he is your lord. All glorious is the princess within her chamber; her gown is interwoven with gold.

—PSALM 45:11,13

This has been a beautiful, crisp December day—my granddaughter Susan's fifth birthday. We celebrated with a party in the park. God allowed a "space" for Kathy and me to open our hearts to each other, as mothers and daughters have a way of doing. Confidences and tears were interspersed with the happy voices of the children playing around us.

A reel unwinds in my memory; little vignettes of a special day. A birthday party in the park; blond, straight, flying hair; laughing eyes blue as the sky; excited tearing of gift wrapping paper; a funny donkey piñata; winter leaves falling silently in the December sun; the quick, staccato voice of anguish; tears followed by peace. The sun beginning to shine hot, bright, and burning. Brown leaves suddenly tipped with gold like the garment of a King's daughter—my Kathy.

And the Psalmist wrote: *All your waves and breakers have swept over me. By day the LORD directs his love, at night his song is with me—a prayer to the God of my life* (Psalm 42:7-8).

Thank You, dear Father, for the blessing of a daughter; for the privilege of being a listener; for the opportunity You give us of showing Your love to one another. Amen.

December 4, 1966

*Send forth your light and your truth, let them
guide me; let them bring me to your holy mountain,
to the place where you dwell. Then will I go to the
altar of God, to God, my joy and my delight.*

—PSALM 43:3-4

God gave me this beautiful psalm of praise for
today—a day destined to be heavy with anxiety and deep
significance. Paul awakened early this morning with great
pain and a high temperature. These recurring attacks,
combined with growing weariness, made it imperative that
we find the cause. Paul entered Baptist Memorial Hospital
this afternoon and extensive tests have begun. I left him
tonight relaxed and comfortable, and he gave me a
cheerful goodbye.

The house seems lonely and empty without him. I have
been thinking about today's scripture, and my heart echoes
this cry . . . I know something of that same longing. I too
stand and gaze wistfully at those tabernacles; my heart is
turned toward the Mount of God. So far away, those
mountains . . . and so high! Will I ever reach them?

*Tonight, Father, I am very frightened. If I am to sing
You my song of praise, I will need Your help.
Is this what you mean by a sacrifice of praise?
Please help me to offer this sacrifice to You. Amen.*

December 5, 1966

The LORD is close to the brokenhearted
and saves those who are crushed in spirit.

—PSALM 34:18

Shock from the doctors' report this afternoon has left me stunned. It is impossible to believe Paul is so ill. Our doctor, with his consultant, came to Paul's room shortly after lunch. They were casual and relaxed . . . one doctor seemed to be having difficulty lighting his pipe. Unfamiliar medical terminology floated around me. Now and then a word penetrated my confusion and clung to the walls of my mind . . . right lung . . . lesion . . . they must be speaking of someone else—not Paul. He looks so healthy since his hospital rest. . . .

When they were gone there was a stillness in the room. It was difficult for us to look at each other. When our eyes met, Paul held out his arms and I went to him. We clung to each other without words. Before the doctors came to Paul's room, they had telephoned Kathy, and in a few minutes she joined us.

Tonight, after returning from the hospital, I made many telephone calls to praying friends across the country. At this moment prayers on Paul's behalf are being lifted to God. I am beginning to feel their strength.

All day I have been clinging to the above scripture. Thank You, dear Lord, for the prayers for Paul, which are rising to You in this very hour. Thank You most of all, Lord, for Your love.

December 6, 1966

*You will restore my life again; from the depths
of the earth you will again bring me up. You will
increase my honor and comfort me once again.*

—PSALM 71:20,21

Today has been a day of waiting . . . waiting for test results.

The entire seventy-first Psalm, particularly the words above, has been a lifeline of hope and comfort to Paul and me today. Years ago, God performed a miracle of healing for Paul. His health was restored and he was given many additional years to live and serve God. We know that God spared his life then, and it is a small thing for Him to do it again. As we wait through these anxious hours, there are blessings coming to us from many different sources.

Father, for every blessing I give You thanks. Above all, for Your presence with us; for Paul's wonderful faith; for his sense of humor, which extends to his nurses and other patients; for the loving support of our children; for the numerous prayers of our friends everywhere which are rising, even now, before Your throne.

*I thank You for our kind doctors—who really care.
Father, You know our hearts and our needs. You know that
Paul and Zada Sherry have never needed You as they
need You now. We look to You for our strength,
for without You, Lord, we cannot stand. Amen.*

91

December 7, 1966

> *I have become like a portent to many,*
> *but you are my strong refuge.*
>
> —PSALM 71:7

Yesterday our physician offered Paul what he believed was his one chance for life: immediate surgery. Paul asked for time to consult with his Lord and Friend.

Today he carefully explained that he made the decision not to have surgery. This, he believes, is God's direction for him. There is no lack of confidence in his doctors—indeed, there is mutual respect. His decision is personal.

His life belongs to God, he reminded me, and if God needs him here, he will live—if not, then God has a better plan for healing.* Thus, without fanfare and in quiet dignity, Paul stepped into a new dimension of faith with the Lord he so deeply loves.

For me, it has been a different matter. In the hospital chapel, I dropped to my knees in a remote corner, my mind racing. I felt numb with grief as cold fingers of terror clutched me. Finally, through sheer willpower, I forced words to my lips and lifted my heart to God. It was then, in great tenderness, the Holy Spirit came to my rescue, and I prayed:

> *My God, Paul is Yours, not mine. Let Your most perfect*
> *will be done in him and in me. May this decision be the*
> *one that will bring the most honor and glory to You.*

---

* Months later Paul's doctor confirmed that, from a medical perspective, Paul had made the right decision.

December 8, 1966

But as for me, I will always have hope;
I will praise you more and more.

—PSALM 71:14

We are rejoicing tonight, because we have Paul home again. We sense that the many prayers of God's people are strengthening us. I am so grateful for the support of family and friends—both near and far away.

As the enemy attempts to "come in like a flood," will You, O God, raise up a standard against him? To keep my mind upon You, Lord, will require my utmost trust. How can I express my love for You? You undergird me with strength, fill my heart with praise, and make peace "my everlasting portion." Who can cheer the soul like You, Lord? You have life for Paul, for You are his life—now and forever. You are my life also, and I must lean hard upon You.

God, we offer You all the love and faith we have, and trust You to multiply it, according to our need, as You did the loaves and fishes by the shores of Galilee. But we are aware, Lord, that it is Your love and mercy, not our faith, which causes You to bless Your people.

December 11, 1966

Search me, O God, and know my heart; test me
and know my anxious thoughts. See if there is any
offensive way in me, and lead me in the way everlasting.

—PSALM 139:23-24

Dear Father, I need Your cleansing and protection, if I am to be a pure instrument of prayer on Paul's behalf. I see areas in my life where I will be most vulnerable to the attacks of the enemy. Keep me, my God, from selfishness, self-pity, possessiveness, anxiety, fear, and doubt of Your love and goodness. Purify my motives and the thoughts and intentions of my heart. In this hour of deep crisis, I long to be found faithful—both as a wife to Paul and in my love for You.

Jesus, Your great love sustains me. I am grateful for the strength You have given me this week, and again I thank You for the prayers on our behalf. We had a phone call from the California church today that they are joining us in prayer. I ask that Your special love and grace be with each one who prays. I praise You, Lord, and I love You with my whole heart.

Jesus, Jesus, I Thee adore, help me
love You more and more.

December 12, 1966

*You have persevered and have endured hardships
for my name, and have not grown weary.*

—REVELATION 2:3

Oh, that I might hear You speak such words to me, my God! Help me also to bear this burden . . . have patience . . . labor . . . and not faint! At present, my "labor" is to trust You and not be afraid. I think at times that I am living in a dream world, and last week's events never happened. However, I have discovered a legacy from those agonizing hours. Deposited deep within my spirit is a peace and joy I have never known. Is it because of the new commitment and surrender I made to You?

I have given You, Lord, my dearest possession: my beloved husband. In this, the season of Your birth, I have given back to You that which is Your own. I am awed by the gratitude I feel in having a gift of such magnitude to give You!

Help me never take the gift back from You. Let me always keep Paul upon Your altar, in Your tender, loving, and healing care. It is his place of greatest safety. And please, dear Father, hold me close also—for I need You so very much.

December 14, 1966

*To him who overcomes and does my will to the end,
I will give authority over the nations.*

—REVELATION 2:26

Now, more than at any time in my life these words of
scripture have a very deep significance for me. No matter
what the days ahead may hold, our lives will never be the
same. Paul's illness has placed us in another dimension of
life; of perspective; of living.

We realize and understand more than ever before, that
life is a sacred gift. For us, life has new value. For the
remainder of our lives Paul and I will walk closer to the
cross, in the power of our Lord's resurrection. In some
ways, this will be exceedingly difficult. In other ways, it
may be easier than ever—for what else do we have to
which to cling?

To be faithful at this time, trusting in God's strength,
as the walls of my former life come tumbling down, will
require a grace and faith which only the Lord Jesus Christ
can provide.

*Dear Father, help me to trust not in my own strength,
but in Yours . . . I give you my life . . . my strength . . .
my all. Help us to overcome. Amen.*

December 15, 1966

Yet you are enthroned as the Holy One;
you are the praise of Israel. In you our fathers put
their trust; they trusted and you delivered them.

—PSALM 22:3,4

The value of praise is disclosed in this scripture. The time when things seem blackest is precisely the time to offer praise to God. Our family was given a new lesson tonight, as God made clear to us that He does indeed love to dwell in the midst of the praise of His people.

Our missionary friend, Wayne Meyers, came today from Mexico City, to encourage us and minister to Paul. We know him to be a mighty man of prayer, and expected something entirely different from what we experienced.

For one hour, Wayne stood by Paul's bedside, praising God . . . no intercession . . . just praise. It was a most unusual experience and very beautiful. We saw that the enemy could not stay in the presence of such an outpouring of adoration and love. Paul's fever left him, and strength returned to his body.

Dear Lord, You have been teaching me for many months the importance of praise. Tonight I saw it demonstrated, and finally I am beginning to understand how much Satan hates to hear You praised.

Thank you, Lord, for ministering to us when we are so in need of Your care. And thank You for Your faithful servant, Wayne. Amen.

97

Rejoice in the Lord always. I will say it again: Rejoice!
Do not be anxious about anything, but in everything . . .
present your requests to God. And the peace of God,
which transcends all understanding, will guard your
hearts and your minds in Christ Jesus.

—PHILIPPIANS 4:4,6,7

Early this morning, I slipped out of the house and went to St. Luke's Episcopal Church for Holy Communion. The above scripture was read . . . not, I think, a coincidence. God seems to be underlining for me the importance of praise. St. Luke's is very near Jack and Kathy's home, so it is convenient for me to attend an occasional service there. The church provides me with a great solace.

Later today, I read and shared this passage of scripture with Paul. I read on through the rest of the chapter, and together we explored God's Word. We felt that our Lord was defining for us the attitude of heart He wishes us to assume in the coming days. We should bring our requests to God with thanksgiving and praise; keep our minds stayed upon Christ; think on positive, not negative things; be content in every situation in which He places us, and find Christ's strength adequate for every need.

How comforting, how blessed, is Your word to us, Lord!
Please give us the strength to live above our
circumstances each day. Thank you.

December 19, 1966

And the angel said unto them, fear not . . .
—LUKE 2:10 KJV

These are timely words God speaks to a troubled world: fear not . . . fear not . . . fear not.

Yet how many can honestly say they have no fear? Can I? "Fear hath torment," wrote St. John. Surely no truer words were ever written! Even as Christmas carols ring out and people finish last minute shopping, much of the world is gripped with fear . . . fear of the future, failure, illness, relationships, and more. The world has not yet heard the angel song, "Fear not." I know now, as I have never known before, that only the Lord Jesus Christ, our mighty Savior, of Whom the angels sang that blessed night so long ago, can save us from the burden of fear.

I know, because He has lifted from me the devastating weight of grief, anxiety, and fear, and has translated me into His Kingdom of peace . . . yes . . . even joy!

Thank you, God, for first delivering me from the bondage of fear through Your grace, through Your supreme gift of Christ, my Lord. And thank You for giving me peace in my present situation. You are a great and merciful God. Amen.

*I am the Living One; I was dead, and
behold I am alive for ever and ever!*

—REVELATION 1:18

Dare a Christian say those words about himself? Not as Christ spoke them, certainly, but every Christian should be able to say with St. Paul, *I have been crucified with Christ and I no longer live, but Christ lives in me. The life I live in the body, I live by faith in the Son of God, who loved me and gave himself for me* (Galatians 2:20). In that context, I too can say: I was dead, yet I live and will be alive forevermore.

In an extraordinary way, this truth is working in Paul's life on another level. Only a few short days ago the dark wings of death were hovering very near. Now it is as though he has been brought back from the dead. I look at him and my heart overflows with gratitude for these precious days our Lord has given us. We breathe again . . . we laugh once more. The sky is so blue . . . the breezes, gentle and caressing. Friends are dear, and life is suddenly real and infinitely beautiful!

*Thank You, Lord, for small miracles
and the simple beauty of life.*

Christmas Eve & Christmas Day 1966

*Today in the town of David a Savior has been
born to you; he is Christ the Lord.*

—LUKE 2:11

Blessed, holy, Christmas Season! What love is being poured out upon us! What joy! What peace! And what precious memories. Our family kneeled together as Paul conducted our own Christmas Eve communion service. This was our granddaughters', Sherry and Susan, first experience of Holy Communion. They looked angelic, kneeling beside us, their childish eyes bright with awe and wonder.

At the exact moment we concluded our little service, we heard the Adams family (all ten of them, plus friends) singing Christmas carols in our front yard! It was God's perfect timing, bringing us His blessings through these special friends. We rushed outdoors to greet them with joy and laughter. Paul hugged each one of them.

Christmas Day has been blessed by our togetherness and the coming and going of various friends. Ken and his family talked to us by telephone this morning, bringing us another joy. And for a long, intimate time, I was curled beside Paul on his bed, holding his hand, listening to Christmas carols on our stereo. Tonight, the family gathered, according to our usual nightly custom, around Paul's bed for prayer and praise.

Dearest Lord Jesus, lovely Lord! Thank You for being born in our hearts again this Christmas Day.

December 29, 1966

The hands of Zerubbabel have laid the foundation of
this temple; his hands will also complete it. Then you
will know that the LORD Almighty has sent me to you.

—ZECHARIAH 4:9

Our living, since we left California only a few short
weeks ago, has been deep and intense. Paul has been to the
gates of death and brought back to renewed life, to find that
the door of service has remained open. We know we do
not go alone, nor in our own strength. In addition to our
Lord's presence, we take with us those who have prayed,
who have stood with us through these difficult days.

As we plan to journey westward once more, we are
sensitive to the privilege we have of carrying God's
reconciling, healing love. There are so many who need to
know what we know . . . hopeless, discouraged individuals,
who need to be told of a personal God Who cares, Whose
power can set them free from oppression and fear.

Dear Father, guide our feet to those who need You.
Open the way, make straight the path into hearts of those
who are hungering and thirsting for You. Lead us to
those who will hear . . . respond . . . and LIVE.

December 31, 1966

*And who knows but that you have come
to royal position for such a time as this?*

—ESTHER 4:14

The year of 1966 will soon be over. It has presented us with many surprises: lessons learned, pain, sorrow, victory. This can be said of any year, of course, but surely for us, this year broke from the conventional pattern into new dimensions of astonishing change! We have been shaken to the depths. All our known securities have been taken from us. But God has remained faithful. Now Paul and I are facing a new year. It will contain challenges and unexplored dimensions of commitment and faith.

As I look back over the year, I can't help but think of the people who have supported us through Paul's illness, both friends and people in the medical profession. And I think of Paul, who has stepped into a new dimension of faith and closeness with his God. How I love and adore that great man of faith and integrity.

Dear Father, I thank You that I am beginning this year with Paul, and it is my prayer that we will end it together. Let this new year be our finest in devotion, love, and service for You.

Thank You, my God, for all that You are to me. May this be a happy new year for You also . . . dwelling in me! Amen.

January 1, 1967

*The LORD is my light and my salvation—whom
shall I fear? The LORD is the stronghold
of my life—of whom shall I be afraid?*

—PSALM 27:1

This is the first day of 1967! It would be very easy for me to be afraid, to focus on difficulties rather than opportunities. The Psalmist may have had some of these very feelings. When he penned the above words, he was reminding himself where his strength was to be found. By relying on that strength he had nothing to fear. Reflecting on these words, I am reminding myself of that very thing!

Paul's health is very fragile. It will require my total dependency upon God if I am to support Paul, as he has asked me to do, in all of his decisions. My ears must be tuned to the voice of God, and I must hear His above all other voices.

Tonight I unexpectedly met one of Paul's physicians. He spoke honestly about Paul's prognosis as he sees it. The encounter left me shaken. I found myself slipping into a pit of hopelessness and fear. It took tremendous willpower to pull myself back from the abyss.

*Help me, dear Father, to hear Your voice. Your Word
is truth. Teach my heart to praise You, Lord, throughout
the coming year, regardless of my circumstances,
for You are always worthy of my praise.*

January 4, 1967

*You yourselves have seen what I did to Egypt,
and how I carried you on eagles' wings.*

—EXODUS 19:4

The Lord did this for Paul and me today. Swiftly, safely, He brought us, over the desert and the mountains, back once more to beautiful California. Al and Elaine met our plane, and we are staying in their home tonight. After we had been here a short time, a few of the church people came by for coffee. I am trying to appreciate our situation and position here in California. The people are so dear.

Lord, the good-byes this morning were very difficult. You knew this, for I cannot deceive You, nor do I want to. You know there is sorrow in my heart tonight because our dear children are so far away.

The path You have chosen for me looks very steep, Lord, and my heart falters at the sight of the boulders which lie ahead. But I love You, Lord, and I have given myself to You. I am looking to Your strength and wisdom for everything I do—concerning Paul, our friends and family, and our ministry.

Tonight, dear Lord, I offer you my praise and thanksgiving for bringing us here safely. Amen.

I will not violate my covenant or
alter what my lips have uttered.

—PSALM 89:34

This morning we moved from Al and Elaine's to a comfortable apartment, which is near our church. Guy, one of our church members, helped us move and get settled. A shopping center is nearby, and I walked to the store for groceries and a few needed items. It is like starting housekeeping all over again . . . and it is fun! After living out of a suitcase for so long, it is great to be settled.

Paul had a difficult time with pain tonight. We read the Bible together, prayed and praised our God. The above scripture was a great help to us, as it reminded us that *we* are covenant people of the Lord! God promises to keep His word concerning us. That thought gives me hope and fills my heart with gratitude.

Paul's trust in His Lord, and his surrender to His purposes are beautiful and complete. I feel weak . . . helpless . . . inadequate by comparison. God must provide strength for us both—and He will.

I offer You my praise, dearest Lord, that "as
our days . . . so shall our strength be." Amen.

January 8, 1967

*Through these he has given us his very great
and precious promises, so that through them
you may participate in the divine nature.*

—2 PETER 1:4

Paul's message today was from this text. At tonight's service he spoke on the Daniel 3, the three Hebrew children in the fiery furnace. I believe God is speaking through him more powerfully than ever. Both of his messages were on faith, and he authenticated his words. It is not easy to preach faith when in pain. But Paul's zeal for God exceeds his physical infirmity. Truly God's strength is being made perfect in his weakness.

However, this has not been an easy day for either of us. Between services, Paul spent much of his time sleeping and resting. I, for the most part, was in prayer for him; much of the time kneeling by his bed as he slept. We are both grateful for this apartment which affords us quietness and privacy. Without Jesus, these hours, for me, would be heavy with anxiety and foreboding. But He sustains and lifts me each time I turn to Him.

*I thank You, dear Lord, and I praise You, that through Your
strength I am not fainting, but growing stronger. Amen.*

January 11, 1967

May integrity and uprightness protect me,
because my hope is in you.

—PSALM 25:21

I am beginning to see that God is working in Paul and me, not only as a couple, but individually as well. I am discovering that the surrender I made to God in the hospital chapel did not end at that time but is an ongoing and deepening experience. The surrender applies not only to Paul's life and health, but also to his work. He has often said that I am "the other half" of his ministry. This is an awesome responsibility, never more so than now.

Not only must I support him in faith, but I must stand back and watch him expend his limited strength. Everything within me cries out to hoard and protect it. This is a fire of purification I have never before experienced. I am aware that God is working on a very deep level in Paul's life also. God has granted us a building—a place to meet temporarily, and I know He is leading every step.

Lord, You are always faithful to show me when
I am getting off the track. You have shown me that
I am trying to work everything out myself instead
of waiting on You. Forgive me. Amen.

January 13, 1967

*But seek first his kingdom and his righteousness,
and all these things will be given to you as well.*

—MATTHEW 6:33

The Amplified Bible translates God's righteousness as "His way of doing and being right." For God says that His ways are not our ways, and His thoughts are not our thoughts (Isaiah 55:8). It is very easy for us to forget these words of the Lord. The world has its own idea of goodness and righteousness, but it is not necessarily the same as God's. Even as Christians, we often spend time and energy doing things that are good, but we miss the *best,* because what we do is not enough. We have made it our work rather than God's.

These quiet days we are spending together are strange and very different from what we expected. We feel that we are accomplishing very little for God. But we are enjoying each other. These are hallowed days Paul and I are spending together. We are loving them . . . the times spent reading our Bibles, praying together, taking walks in the bright California sunshine, enjoying the tranquillity and privacy of this little apartment—all beautiful gifts from our loving Father.

*We thank You, dear Lord, for the blessings You are giving
us . . . now . . . at this time . . . in this place. Amen.*

*Let us not become weary in doing good, for at the
proper time we will reap a harvest if we do not give up.*

—GALATIANS 6:9

The Holy Spirit guides me often to this scripture these
days. I am becoming more and more impressed with the
truth that God's idea of well doing and ours may be poles
apart. Well doing in God's eyes may appear to others as
doing nothing. Having done all we know to do, then we
are to *stand,* as St. Paul wrote to the church in Ephesus.

Just stand? Do nothing? Only trust? And believe God?
This is God's idea of doing well? Yes! And it often requires
more grace and fortitude than to be actively engaged in a
great project. For the greatest work of God is often
accomplished in solitude and darkness, hidden from the
eyes of the world.

Hidden with God, the little seed is planted in the dark
ground, then it begins to germinate, and tiny sprouts are
formed. In God's time they appear above ground and
continue their growth. But the most important activity goes
on unseen by human eyes, alone in the darkness with God.

*Thank You, Father, for Your silent,
unseen work within us. Amen.*

January 16, 1967

But the crowds learned about it and followed him.
He welcomed them and spoke to them about the kingdom
of God, and healed those who needed healing.

—LUKE 9:11

This scripture must surely be for Paul and me today! Paul has been in pain, and I have had the worst case of sinusitis I've had in months. Both of us have spent most of the day in bed. We could refrain from giving praise to God. However, there are always things for which to praise our Lord, no matter how gloomy the situation.

I love the Scriptures because they are so honest. They allow a child of God to express what he really feels. This is especially evident in the Psalms. David always expressed how he actually felt: Sometimes he was discouraged and defeated, sometimes he was in the depths of despair. At other times, in the midst of difficult situations, he spoke sternly to his own soul. No wonder that he was called "a man after God's own heart" in spite of his imperfections. David knew how to be honest with God, and God loved him for it. He could honestly lament, honestly repent, and honestly praise God.

I love You, Lord, and praise You because You are
always so dear and wonderful to me. Amen.

*You will drink from the brook, and I have ordered
the ravens to feed you there. The ravens brought
him bread and meat in the morning and bread and
meat in the evening, and he drank from the brook.*

—1 KINGS 17:4,6

It rained all day, and we have been shut in with each
other—and God—in blissful solitude. No one came to see
us, nor did the phone ring. It had to be a day planned by
God solely for our benefit and joy! Paul has rested and
relaxed in preparation for tomorrow's services.

I remember how intensely we have longed for a place
where we could have privacy and quiet. God has provided
it for us, but who could have dreamed it would be in
California? Truly His ways are not our ways, or His
thoughts our thoughts! Paul needs days like this . . . he
must have them to carry out his work. For a period of
time, it seems our Lord is ministering to us. He is
providing bountifully for our needs, and we are hidden
under His wings. We are resting quietly, in His love.

*Even as You cared for Your prophet, Elijah, so are You
caring for us, O God. We give You our thanks and praise.*

January 22, 1967

*How good and pleasant it is when
brothers live together in unity!*

—PSALM 133:1

Today we have been especially blessed by our Christian family. How wonderful it is to have the opportunity to be and speak with other Christians! There's a unique and beautiful understanding among those who believe in Christ. They minister to us from near and far—miles make no difference.

This afternoon a number of our friends from the Davis church telephoned to assure us of their continuing love and prayers. Tonight our church had a surprise for us—giving us gifts, groceries, and items to help us get started. Again and again we are experiencing our Father's love through others. In a "strange and alien" land, we find His loving children caring for our needs.

We thank You, Father, for Your love poured out to us through these, Your children. Paul was strong in Your strength today, and Your people were blessed through his ministry. Even though I know You and love You, and should not be surprised at Your goodness and love, I am amazed as I watch You work through Your servant, Paul.

**Thank You, dear Lord, for all I am seeing You do . . .
and also for those things I can't see. Amen.**

January 27, 1967

*This is what the LORD says—your Redeemer,
the Holy One of Israel: "I am the LORD
your God, who teaches you what is best for you,
who directs you in the way you should go."*

—ISAIAH 48:17

This has been a good day for Paul. It was brightened by a wonderful, loving letter from our son, Richard. It thrilled and warmed our hearts, and Paul wept as he read it.

All parents know there are areas in which they fail their children. We are not like God. We do not see so clearly the sensitivity and talents, nor do we always have the wisdom to know how to bring forth the gifts given them by God. Praying parents make the difference, for God has made special promises in reference to our children . . . among them this wonderful assurance: *I will contend with those who contend with you, and your children I will save* (Isaiah 49:25).

This son of ours, because of his unique and sensitive spirit, has caused us anxiety and sometimes pain. Through the years, and across the miles from us, God has been leading him and teaching him, even as the above scripture promises. Families are important to God.

*Thank You, Father, for our children, and for
this beloved son. Thank You for the beauty
You are bringing forth in his life. Amen.*

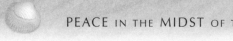

January 28, 1967

*Praise be to the Lord, to God our Savior,
who daily bears our burdens.*

—PSALM 68:19

This is a good scripture for a dreary, rainy day. Every life has hours or days of boredom and loneliness. There are days when it "rains on our parade." But God tells us that He daily *loads* us with blessings and benefits. His servant Jeremiah expressed this thought beautifully with the words: *Because of the LORD's great love we are not consumed, for his compassions never fail. They are new every morning; great is your faithfulness* (Lamentations 3:22-23).

So—no matter the weather and no matter the circumstances—God's mercies come to us every day, and His praise should be continually on our lips. When it is not easy to praise and be thankful, our praise becomes a sacrifice. This is pleasing to God and brings Him joy, because it reveals the depth and sincerity of our love for Him.

Dear Father, for companionship with my beloved, for shelter, food, friends, dear children, life, salvation, cleansing, and right-standing with You . . . for eyes to see, ears to hear, a work to do for You, for Your Word . . . for all these, and much more, I give You thanks.

**Forgive me for the benefits I fail to acknowledge
or even notice! Help me to become more aware
of Your blessings in my life. Amen.**

115

January 31, 1967

But you, O LORD, be not far off;
O my Strength, come quickly to help me.

—PSALM 22:19

Today has been a day of vigil, prayer and quiet waiting. Paul has slept most of the day. I have been amazed through all of these weeks how free he has been of medication. He has taken almost nothing for pain and this can only be God's grace and mercy to His servant. I thank Him for His blessing in this area. I am so grateful.

The sun has been out again today and I walked to the shopping center and bought Valentines for our "little ones" back in Texas. It is the last of January. We began this month in San Antonio with our loved ones there. How different our life is now—how quiet! We are shut in, alone with our faithful and merciful God.

I am still confident of this: I will see the goodness of the LORD in the land of the living. Wait for the LORD; be strong and take heart and wait for the LORD (Psalm 27:13-14).

Dear Lord, help me to be strong, to take heart,
and to wait—to wait on You. Amen.

February 2, 1967

*But the Counselor, the Holy Spirit, whom the Father
will send in my name, will teach you all things
and will remind you of everything I have said to you.*

—JOHN 14:26

Elaine came by tonight and stayed until eleven thirty . . .
praying with us and encouraging us. God bless her!

I am learning so much as I keep this journal day by
day. God is teaching me many things about Himself. He
seems to be telling me to keep on writing in my journal—
that these lessons and experiences are important, not for
me only—but for others who may face similar situations.
The things we learn on our journey through life are never
just for us. They are to be shared.

So . . . what does one do when a dear one is ill? First
of all, I am learning the importance of total surrender, so
far as is humanly possible, to the Father's will. We keep
our hearts free from self-condemnation and guilt through
repentance and confession. It is important also to keep in
mind that God is sovereign in all things. Our loved one's
life belongs to Him. He has the supreme right to do what
he will with that life. This surrender is not an easy one, but
with God's help it is possible.

*I thank You, dear Lord, for the grace You have given me
to surrender my dearest possession to You. Amen.*

February 4, 1967

Keep me as the apple of your eye;
hide me in the shadow of your wings.

—PSALM 17:8

I am learning that when I am tempted to doubt God's promises, I should run quickly to Jesus. Otherwise, before I can gather my spiritual resources, I am swept away in a sea of anguish, fear, and unbelief.

We choose who will be in control in every situation. We can choose to walk with God in faith, or succumb to the negative realm, which is Satan's playground. Under the shadow of God's sheltering love, standing upon the rock of His faithful promises, we can look Satan in the eye with confidence, *knowing who we are in God.* We are the very "apple of His eye!"

When we truly understand His power and His presence in our lives, we can truly trust that He is working in all the situations of our lives. And if we let Him, he will lead us and guide us in all situations.

God, show me when I'm not trusting You, and quickly
lead me to Your path, Your way and in Your will.

February 7, 1967

I can do everything through him who gives me strength.
—PHILIPPIANS 4:13

God alone may understand what I mean when I write: this is my finest hour. It is not said in arrogance, but in the deep awareness that I have never faced a greater challenge, I have never been more alone, yet never have I been more adequate in God. Day by day, hour by hour, His strength comes to me, to be poured into Paul's great need.

Last night was his most difficult night. Only with God's grace can I see him in such pain, and remain committed to God's "ultimate intention." Yet Paul does not want my apprehension. He wants my strength, as it comes to me from God; he wants my faith to strengthen his; he wants my laughter and love; he wants to hear my songs of praise to God.

I have, throughout my life, always had someone— especially Paul—to lean on, or turn to. Now there is no one. The days pass, no one calls or comes by; no one close to us knows how to pray with me. God has become my strength, my faith, my all.

Lord, in Your great compassion and love, please make Yourself known to me. Thank You for being my faithful companion.

February 8, 1967

*He asked you for life, and you gave it
to him—length of days, for ever and ever.*

—PSALM 21:4

Father, I present the words of this Psalm to you as my evening prayer. Paul does not ask life for himself alone, but for the purpose of completing his work for You. But You are not a harsh master, whipping and driving Your servants as slaves. You have called us Your friends, and it is in this relationship that Paul has offered himself to be spent for You. He is identified with Your purpose for this sinful, dying world.

Last December, on that terrible night when I first knew how sick Paul was, You comforted me with these words of the Psalmist: *Even when I am old and gray, do not forsake me, O God, till I declare your power to the next generation, your might to all who are to come* (Psalm 71:18). This is Paul's desire, Father: that You might pour Your love and power through him for as long as You need him. My heart tells me that You will answer this prayer in a far greater way than I can imagine.

Keep me steadfast in my devotion to You. Forgive all my sins, and lead me in the way of Your righteousness and truth. Keep me strong for Paul. Amen.

February 10, 1967

Give thanks to the LORD, for he is good.
His love endures forever.

—PSALM 136:1

Today I attended the World Day of Prayer at the Lutheran Church. After a long week of pain and hours of prayer, Paul is definitely better today. This morning he got his hair cut, and this afternoon we drove up the Sacramento River, a beautiful drive in the bright winter sunshine. These days, when we can, we are enjoying the simple things of life—a haircut, a drive. Does the sun really shine brighter on the days he feels better?

We received a letter from a young couple in Oklahoma today, enclosing money. There is so much love pouring into us, and many, many prayers. They are like a thousand hands . . . a thousand voices reaching out to us! We briefly attended a Sunday School party tonight in the home of one of our church families. How thankful we are for God's graciousness to us through the people in our lives.

O Father! We are so very grateful for this respite from pain.
We thank and praise You for Your grace and favor upon us.
Hold us, O God, steadfastly to Your purposes. Amen.

> *Then suddenly, the Lord you are seeking will come*
> *to his temple; the messenger of the covenant, whom*
> *you desire, will come, says the* LORD *Almighty.*

—MALACHI 3:1

Paul has been quite sick today with a high temperature. We think he may have a cold. Tonight I am at my lowest ebb. The walls of our little apartment seem to be closing in. I didn't go to mid-week service for fear of leaving Paul alone.

I have so much to be thankful for, and yet, if I am honest, I must record that I am desperately lonely. It seems I have reached the very lowest rung of the ladder—I am at the end of my resources, and God seems very far away. If I had someone to talk to it would help, or someone to pray with me, for I need prayers tonight as much as Paul.

This is such a gloomy page! I cannot stop here but must close the day with praise to God. I can say with the words of Job, *When men are brought low and you say, "lift them up!" then he will save the downcast* (Job 22:29).

> *Father, I am looking to You for answers tonight,*
> *and for lifting up. I am on sinking sand tonight.*
> *Will You reach out with Your hand and lift me,*
> *please, to "the Rock that is higher than I"?*

February 15, 1967

He will call upon me, and I will answer him; I will be with him in trouble, I will deliver him and honor him.

—PSALM 91:15

This morning I went for an early walk. I felt a desperate need to be outdoors. I walked rapidly, enjoying the crispness of the air. Suddenly, as I walked, I felt praise for God welling up from deep within me. I completed my walk in thanksgiving and praise—not knowing why.

When I returned to the apartment, Paul told me Kenneth and Kathy had called. Ken was spending a few hours in San Antonio with Kathy, and asked me to return his call. When he answered my call, his first words were: "Mother, when are you coming home? We think it is time." As I turned from the phone I knew God had been speaking to me through our son. My prayer of last night had been answered.

Today I have seen Paul through new eyes. God protected me until His time for us to leave had come. Tomorrow afternoon at five o'clock we will be flying back to Texas. It seems right to leave now. The responsibility of a church is too much for Paul.

Father, I thank You for the beautiful hours
You have given us here. Oh! how I thank You!
Please bless the work that we have done here. Amen.

> *He reached down from on high and took*
> *hold of me; he drew me out of deep waters.*
>
> —PSALM 18:16

Night before last, I read in Job that "there is a lifting up"—and there is! Today, Guy and Loretta, a young couple in our church, took us to San Francisco, where we caught the plane for our return to Texas. They came early to help Paul get ready and to help us pack. Then, they told us to just walk out of the apartment and they would pack and ship our belongings. What loving kindness!

It was wonderful to feel the plane lifting us up . . . up . . . and out over the sparkling waters of the Pacific, down the long coastline, past Carmel by the Sea, and then over the mountains to Texas. People on the plane were extremely kind to us. Paul and I flew through the night, hand in hand, relaxed and at peace, scarcely speaking. Before we knew it we were landing at the San Antonio airport, and there was our Kathy. Then home to Jack, and sleeping Sherry and Susan. We are home!

Thank You, my Father, for Your great love and grace,
and for Your perfect plan for our lives. Amen.

February 17, 1967

*Now to him who is able to do immeasurably
more than all we ask or imagine, according
to his power that is at work within us.*

—EPHESIANS 3:20

All my loneliness is being replaced by overflowing love, as friends gather here to pray, and to bless us. One by one they come, hour after hour, lifting our spirits. Some bring food—and all bring the healing gift of God's love. Rivers of peace are seeping into our parched souls through these dear friends. Kenneth flew up from the Valley and is here with us to share in these blessed hours. Truly this is the ministry of the Body of Christ. In the book of Galatians, it says, "Carry each other's burdens." These loving people are doing just that, figuratively and literally.

O God, I can never cease to praise You for Your timing! You have brought us to the green pastures, beside the still waters. After all the anguish of uncertainty, You have shown Yourself faithful.

Dear God, let Your healing love continue until Your wholeness and salvation are extended to every member of our family. I thank You, my God, that You have lifted me above grief and anxiety—into Your rest.

February 18, 1967

The LORD gives strength to his people;
the LORD blesses his people with peace.

—PSALM 29:11

These are golden hours! Our son, Richard, arrived from Michigan and our family is complete. This has been a wonderful day of togetherness. It is a very special time to have both our sons here. We can almost feel the beat of angel's wings about us—so real is our Lord's presence.

Paul is weak, but has no pain and can enjoy the companionship and fun. We both stand in awe at the redemptive love at work in our family. Who can doubt the faithfulness of our High Priest, Who lives to make intercession for us? When we pray, we join our prayers with His. Many prayers are being answered today.

Sometimes it seems to take God a long time to answer prayers for a family, but as we continue to pray, God is at work, whether we see the evidence or not. Often He works in loving patience, weaving His pattern of redemption . . . not only in one life, but in many. Later we are amazed at how much has been accomplished.

My God, I can only bow before You and acknowledge Your hand upon us all! Thank You.

February 20, 1967

*By myself I can do nothing; I judge only as
I hear, and my judgment is just, for I seek
not to please myself but him who sent me.*

—JOHN 5:30

If our Lord found it necessary to say this, expressing
His total dependence upon His Father, how much more do
I? I know I can do nothing of myself, nor can I be strong,
or have faith, without God's help. It is strange to realize
that we cannot even give to God unless He gives to us first!

There are times when I look at Paul's frailty and my
heart breaks. Then I remember why Peter failed when he
attempted to walk to his Lord over the waves. It is only by
looking steadily at Jesus that I can have His vision. In
looking at Him, He gives me new eyes with which to see.
At these times I can see beyond the frail body of my
husband to his emerging spirit. There is an almost ethereal
quality about him. The Holy Spirit at times seems to
emanate from him almost visibly. His face frequently has a
radiance that is very lovely.

Ken left today. He has been a tower of strength. God's
grace to our family has been very great.

*O God! You are so wonderful! I thank You for
lifting me above grief and anxiety into Your rest.*

February 21, 1967

My comfort in my suffering is this:
Your promise preserves my life.

—Psalm 119:50

This is such a powerful scripture! Our Lord Jesus said, "My words are Spirit and they are life." Paul and I are finding this to be true as we search and cling to God's Word each day. By it we are being purified and strengthened. Our Lord has promised that His Word would do this very thing for us. Through God's Word our minds are renewed and we are built up in Him. It is very important that we remain humble and sensitive to God's spirit. The Lord Jesus longs to be the companion of every traveler who embarks upon the road with Him. When He is walking with us, *He takes the heaviest part of the burden.*

Paul is much stronger . . . stronger each day. His fellow minister, Ervin Veale, came to see us today. This dear friend added his joy and faith to ours. One week ago tonight I was in the quagmire of discouragement. In a matter of hours, God easily and quickly rescued us and brought us to this haven of rest and peace.

Thank You, precious Lord, that You never fail us!

February 28, 1967

But as for you, the LORD took you and brought you
out of the iron-smelting furnace, out of Egypt, to
be the people of his inheritance, as you now are.

—DEUTERONOMY 4:20

This, O God, You have done for us! You have brought
us into a new place of waiting. This time we have left the
desert and are dwelling beside the quiet streams of Your
healing love. We have found You equally precious in both
places! In this place to which You have led us, we await
our inheritance, which we hope may be healing for Paul,
and opportunities of service for You.

Paul has felt better and better, no doubt in part from
the love of those who are close with us. It seems that God
is extending his days—and giving life to his days.

This is my prayer to you, today, Lord:

Praise the Lord, O my soul; all my inmost being,
praise his holy name. Praise the Lord, O my soul, and
forget not all his benefits—who forgives all your sins and
heals all your diseases, who redeems your life from the pit
and crowns you with love and compassion (Psalm 103:1-4).

Ask . . . seek . . . knock.

—LUKE 11:9

Dear Lord, I need Your strength, wisdom, patience, faith, and especially Your love! Indeed, I know myself to be utterly poverty stricken, without Your grace and help. Help me, my God, through the experiences of each day, to learn more of You. Help me not to waste my time in vain imaginations or regrets. Keep my heart fixed upon You, for it is so prone to wander!

I present Paul to You tonight for all of his needs. I have my needs; he has his. Our finances are more limited now. We do not have a place to live, and we are dependent upon our children. We are grateful for the love we have received in this home, but as parents, we have concern for them also. We do not want to disrupt their home life or be a burden to them. They are looking for a larger home to buy. We are looking for a place we may call ours, so that all of us may have the privacy we need.

I present these needs to You, Father, with thanksgiving, that You will meet them, in Your own wonderful way, above all our expectations. Amen.

March 6, 1967

My comfort in my suffering is this:
Your promise preserves my life.

—PSALM 119:50

Dear Father, I am very grateful that years ago You guided Paul and me to Your Word and showed to us its reality and truth. You gave us faith to believe it *as* Your Word. The scripture for today is timely for Paul, because his consolation indeed, is in Your Word. It has revived him and is giving him new life. Today was much easier for him than yesterday. All of his days here are better than any day in California.

Father, I do not believe I have thanked You for the holy calling You have given me of ministering to him for You. I consider it a great privilege. It is a joy to me, and brings a fulfillment I have not known before. I do not mean to sound super-spiritual or pious, nor am I saying it is easy. I am saying I count it as a vocation, ordained of You . . . and in humility I acknowledge it as such.

May I be constant, faithful and devoted to this calling—for love of You, O God, and for love of Paul. I thank You that You have considered me worthy. Amen.

131

 *March 7, 1967*

*For my own sake, for my own sake, I do this.
How can I let myself be defamed? I am he;
I am the first and I am the last.*

—Isaiah 48:11,12

Sometimes we think we must defend God's honor and reputation. We attempt to "demonstrate" or prove His Word. We become tense if our prayers are not answered immediately. We are fearful that unbelievers will interpret God as being unfaithful, uncaring, or indifferent.

Yet our God stands and acts on His own power. He does not need to be proved, nor does He need anyone to defend Him. When we pray, when we face life's sometimes-tragic events, it is a mistake to think as if God is on trial.

I wonder, at times, at our human condition and our standing before God. Can we trust Him fully, even in the dark with no apparent light to guide us, because we are assured of His integrity? Do we know His character well enough to have confidence in Him?

I ask myself these questions.

*Lord, in my darkness, I lift my eyes to You.
Please, show me Your light.*

March 8, 1967

How can I repay the LORD for all his goodness to me
—PSALM 116:12

Your gifts to us, O Lord, are exceedingly great! But there would be no real joy in them if they did not include You. For all earthly joys and pleasures are intensified when we are walking with the Giver. The sky is bluer, the birds sing sweeter, earthly loves and relationships become holy and precious, and everything in life comes into clearer, sharper focus.

At times, it is difficult to know what's true and worth our time and concern, and what is not. I often wonder about reality—what's real in this life.

I know that we can only discern what is true from what is false through You, for You have said, "I am the Truth," and it is through You that the scales fall from our eyes and receive our true sight. We gain a new perspective, and can better evaluate the things of earth and appreciate more fully the things eternal.

Please give me eyes to see and ears to hear what is real and vital to this life. Thank You for Your Holy Spirit, the Comforter. Amen.

 *March 9, 1967*

*Do not be seized with alarm and
struck with fear; only keep on believing.*

—MARK 5:36 AMP

I need to keep this admonition before me constantly.
There are times when present circumstances are like a vise,
constricting me. I feel stifled—there is no way of escape.

It is, I am sure, a tremendous thrill, an exhilarating
experience, to climb the highest peak of a mountain range.
What a view that must be! There would be endless vistas
stretching ahead . . . peak upon peak of magnificent
splendor. The discipline and pain of the climb would fade
or would seem as nothing in comparison with the reward.

This is my own desire and longing as I climb my
mountain. I do not want regrets, nor do I want to give the
enemy opportunity to penetrate my spiritual armor,
depriving me of what is mine. There are two dangers, I am
discovering, in such a climb. One is to look back down the
trail I have traveled, the other is to look too far ahead. It
has to be one step at a time, with the confidence that the
Guide I have chosen to climb with me never fails to reach
His goal.

*Father, I thank You for the mountains.
I give You praise for You have said You would
make even our mountain a way to You!*

March 12, 1967

*In righteousness you will be established: Tyranny
will be far from you; you will have nothing to fear.
Terror will be far removed; it will not come near you.*

—ISAIAH 54:14

Paul and I drove to Somerset again this morning where
he preached for his friend, Jesse Long. I tried not to let the
fear of over-taxing his strength spoil the joy he felt in
preaching again. Using his voice weakens him. Over and
over I see God's strength being manifested through his
weakness. Often it is apparent when individuals come to
seek his advice and prayer. Sometimes young people come
and weep because they feel the tug of God upon their
hearts as He speaks to them through Paul.

*Father, thank You that Lent has not come and gone
without your showing me something I might do for You.
You have shown me something that I might offer You as a
gift of my love. It was not fasting, nor the usual physical
denials, but something which is the very essence of all that
I am. I give to You my wifely inclination to hover and be
protective when You are using Paul to minister to others.
This is the one thing that will keep me constantly leaning
upon You.*

**O Lord, I thank You for helping me
to be what I long to be in You!**

When I called, you answered me;
you made me bold and stouthearted.

—PSALM 138:3

O Lord, I have no strength but Yours, and even when I am most needing it, I cannot always receive it. You are always giving; Your strength is always available. Help me in my inability to receive.

My will is flabby, my faith weak. But You are the Finisher of my faith as well as its Beginning. Your Word is true and You are faithful. So I rejoice in Your faithfulness, even as I confess to You my inconsistency.

Look upon Your servant, Lord, and hear my cry. You have promised to bring me to my "desired haven," so all I need to do is set my sails. The winds of Your Spirit will speed me over the waves and bring me where I cannot bring myself. No need for a motor or oars for rowing— nor do I need a compass to chart my course. I look up and see the sails billowing in the breeze. You are here, and all is well.

Father, make me Your child, bold and stouthearted, for I am calling on You today.

March 16, 1967

*I will tell of the kindnesses of the LORD,
the deeds for which he is to be praised,
according to all the Lord has done for us.*

—ISAIAH 63:7

This was a good day for Paul! We drove to our beloved "hill country." When we started to get into the car, I offered to drive, but Paul slid behind the wheel with the words, "I want to drive." His hands were steady upon the wheel, and there was a look of contentment upon his face. Soon the city was behind us, and we were heading for the springtime beauty of the Texas hills.

The bright sunshine and the warm spring air added to the reliving of many happy memories and were as wine in our veins! What joy—what heaven—to be riding quietly along together again, in the blessed oneness of each other!

It might seem a very small event to some, but to us it was charged with deep significance. It represented added days of companionship . . . a gift of God . . . when only a short time ago it seemed to be over; something we would never experience again.

After a while, Paul quietly turned the car around and headed back to San Antonio. The late afternoon sun, playing hide-and-seek among the hills, cast long shadows across the road as we drove.

Thank You, Father.

> *In his great mercy he has given us*
> *new birth into a living hope through the*
> *resurrection of Jesus Christ from the dead.*
>
> —1 PETER 1:3

Kathy and Jack have gone to Monterrey, Mexico, and Paul and I are keeping the grandchildren. Today we so enjoyed our two little girls, Sherry and Susan.

Paul and I have been reading the Bible together, over and over, these last months. We have read the Gospels, and today we are reading the words of our friend, Peter. These are memorable hours together. I love to have Paul share his insights into God's Word with me.

O God! You know the ache of it! You are our High Priest . . . touched with the feelings of our infirmities, heartaches and sorrows. Yet Your Word, through Peter, encourages us.

> **Dear Lord, I cannot deny the pain You know**
> **is mine. But I offer it to You that it may be a**
> **holy grief, mixed with joy at Your faithfulness.**

March 20, 1967

Sorrowful, yet always rejoicing; poor yet making
many rich; having nothing, and yet possessing everything.

—2 CORINTHIANS 6:10

I understand the meaning of these words now as never before. It is true, sometimes I am very sorrowful, yet I do not grieve as one having no hope. I certainly do not have much security, by the world's standard, yet I am seeing lives maturing and deepening, and being touched for Christ.

"Poor" in material possessions, we are finding ourselves "rich" toward God. Earthly possessions cannot compare with the peace that comes from being in the will of God. Gold cannot compare to the light of His smile, nor can it bring fulfillment, as can the knowledge one is being used for His purposes. And there is no privilege greater than that of standing by a man who is called of God, who is yielded to His purposes—even unto death.

However, being poor and obscure is not the secret to happiness. It is only through being in the will of God, of giving ourselves fully to Him daily (and sometimes, it seems, moment by moment), that we will experience true peace.

O Jesus, my Lord! In the day of Your revealing,
multitudes shall worship and adore You, and
kings shall cast their crowns at Your feet!

March 23, 1967

Simon Peter answered him, "Lord, to whom shall we go?
You have the words of eternal life."

—JOHN 6:68

Dear God, these are my words to You today. For there is nothing in this world that makes sense or has any meaning outside of You. And yet, Your purposes are often veiled. Sometimes it seems we know nothing at all!

Seeing another suffer, especially one you hold so dear and so close, brings one to the inevitable question: "Why?" I understand that we live in a fallen world, full of hardship, trials and, yes, suffering. St. Paul, in first Corinthians 13, gives one of the greatest analogies for our present condition: *Now we see but a poor reflection as in a mirror; then we shall see face to face. Now I know in part; then I shall know fully, even as I am fully known.*

I suppose at times every believer in You asks himself, "Am I crazy?" Abraham must have asked himself that question as he left everything for a "land he knew not of." And yet, Lord, what keeps us pressing on, no matter how foolish it may appear except that Your Spirit draws us?

Help me Father, to keep looking to You. Draw near, dear God, and grant me Your peace.

March 27, 1967

*And now these three remain: faith, hope and love.
But the greatest of these is love.*

—1 CORINTHIANS 13:13

The word hope has new meaning for me today. Paul and I looked at some lovely mobile homes, and we dreamed again. We hoped and planned. Is this the next step in God's plan for us? These days, it is so difficult to know for sure. One step at a time . . . that's as much as we can take.

We do have a great desire to have our own home once more. We also went to look at a new home Jack and Kathy are planning to buy. Changes come, for life is always, relentlessly pressing us into new decisions. It is never static. However, the results of our decisions have a new dimension when we are committed to God's purposes. The balance is altered, even when there is a mistake in judgment, because God works all things for good to those who love Him and are called according to *His* purpose (Romans 8:28). We trust that God is guiding us, even now, as we seek out our options.

*Dear Jesus . . . Holy God! Guide our steps into
Your eternal purposes, and we will be satisfied. Amen.*

April 1, 1967

To the weak I became weak, to win the weak.
I have become all things to all men so that
by all possible means I might save some.

—1 CORINTHIANS 9:22

Paul is very tired tonight, so I am staying with him in our room, rather than attending the evening lecture. Friends have been in and out to visit and to pray. It is here by Paul's side that I find peace and rest. I am grateful for the privilege of ministering God's love and mine to this dear man. I find a unique joy in it, even though a "sword pierces my heart."

We are on the third floor of the lodge, and the wind sings us a special hymn of praise as it rustles through the trees. Darkness has fallen and everything is quiet, except for the noises of God's little creatures, settling down for the night. In the distance, down at the auditorium, I can hear people singing. The haunting strains of the nine-fold "Hallelujah" float through our windows, bringing us a sense of comfort and peace.

Father, in this holy quietness, alone with You, I offer You my praise. The words of Your servant David echo within my heart: "Let my prayer be set forth before Thee as incense; and the lifting up of my hands as the evening sacrifice." Amen.

April 4, 1967

Praise the LORD, all you nations; extol him, all you peoples.
For great is his love toward us, and the faithfulness
of the LORD endures forever. Praise the LORD.

—PSALM 117

Dear God, my own dear Father:

What can I render to You for all Your benefits? All our provision comes from You, and through these wonderful people You have given us a full scholarship to this marvelous retreat!

Today Paul was able to eat normally, and even enjoyed the food at the outdoor barbecue, asking for a second helping! We are being overwhelmed with Your love coming to us through Your people. Thank You for Your faithfulness, for the love that endures.

Father, I am still keeping my covenant with You and with Paul. I am standing in faith before You for His healing. Day by day his strength comes from You. Wherever You may lead us, Father, we want to go, to share and witness for You. We are expendable for Your purposes. We desire to follow as Your Spirit leads.

April 5, 1967

And I will restore to you the years. . . .

—JOEL 2:25 KJV

We are alone tonight in the lodge. The retreat ended at noon today. This morning during the sharing time, Paul spoke briefly about how God is working in our lives. The good-byes were difficult.

We have been standing on the balcony, just outside our room. The warm, night air enveloped us in its loving embrace as we thanked God for His goodness to us. We stayed for awhile, silently drinking in the beauty of the night; watching the stars, gleaming like diamonds in the Texas sky . . . listening to the river sounds nearby.

Tonight we ate dinner with our hill-country friends, Christine and Frank Thomas. Then God's next step was revealed to us as a beautiful surprise. During the week, unknown to us, arrangements were made to provide us with another home. Mildred Edmondson has a cottage, next to her own home, on the Guadalupe River. She has offered it to us for as long as we want to stay!

How could I have dreamed such a short time ago, when praying for a home, that God would provide such a place as this?

> *God . . . our loving, tender, Heavenly Father!*
> *These hills have a special significance for Paul and me.*
> *I will lift up my eyes to the hills, where does my help*
> *come from? From You, dear Lord. From You.*

144

April 5, 1967

Many waters cannot quench love;
rivers cannot wash it away.

—SONG OF SOLOMON 8:7

While here at the retreat, Paul and I made love to each other. It was wonderful and fulfilling for us both. The intimacy brought us comfort and a sense of nearness, which we needed, and have not experienced for some time.

I was aware that Paul was reaching desperately for life and normality. I was also aware of his anger—anger and frustration against the insidious disease that has made slow, but deliberate, inroads into his life. He is a man, strong and vital of spirit. He still longs to participate in life but does not have the strength.

Later, we clung to each other, numb and inarticulate. Our pain was too deep for words. After he was asleep, I lay in his arms, staring into the darkness, as cold waves of fear swept over me. I could see nothing to relieve the blackness—not so much as a faint outline or glimmer of light. The night was very dark indeed.

Through Your word, You speak to me: *Even the darkness will not be dark to you; the night will shine like the day, for darkness is as light to you* (Psalm 139:12).

God, help me to see Your light, illuminating the heavy darkness that seems to surround me now. Amen.

April 6, 1967

And my God will meet all your needs
according to his glorious riches in Christ Jesus.

—PHILIPPIANS 4:19

We are back in San Antonio this afternoon to pack and prepare to go back to our new home in the hills. We feel confident this is God's place for us at the present time. The river, the beauty, and the quiet are His prescription—only He knew how to fill it.

To walk with God is better than to have all the wealth the world has to offer. Why do we ever hesitate to trust the Master of the universe? The cattle on a thousand hills are His, and He knows the individuals who will respond to His gentle suggestions for the needs of others.

It is nice to be back in this home tonight, and to be welcomed by squeals of joy from our two little girls, as well as by the warmth and love of Jack and Kathy. How rich we are!

Lord, how can I ever thank You for this amazing
answer to prayer? You are a great God, worthy of
all my trust and praise. Help me to grow in my
faith that I might serve You fully. Amen.

April 9, 1967

Follow my example, as I follow the example of Christ.
—1 CORINTHIANS 11:1

The above words challenge me! I ask myself if my union with Christ is deep enough for me to say such words to another. They could be the very epitome of arrogance unless I understand and have experienced what St. Paul wrote to the Galatians: *I have been crucified with Christ and I no longer live, but Christ lives in me. The life I live in the body I live by faith in the Son of God, who loved me and gave himself for me* (Galatians 2:20).

Sometimes it takes a long time before the truth penetrates a believer's heart and mind that Jesus Christ has taken residence within and desires to live out His life *through* us.

Jack, Kathy, and the children brought us to our hill country home today, and helped us get settled. Since the cottage is furnished there was little to be done. Tonight we are alone in this heavenly place. We have been sitting on our screened-in porch, overlooking the river, listening to our favorite music. It has been a full day.

> *Father dear, we know this is Your gift to us.*
> *Grant that we may use these days wisely and well.*
> *We pray for healing of body, mind, and spirit as*
> *we live in this delightful little cottage with You.*

April 10, 1967

Be still, and know that I am God.

—PSALM 46:10

This is exactly what we have done today. We have quietly and simply known that God is!

It has been a beautiful day: watching the birds; the deer feeding across the river; the wild turkeys; the shadows and reflections on the river. I bought Paul bait and a fishing license this morning. He walked down to the river and fished, which is one of his favorite forms of recreation.

It is difficult to realize that we have been given the great privilege of living in this beautiful place. So far, I can only sit back, take it in, and enjoy it all. It has seemed almost sinful to do anything except absorb the beauty around me, and how very lovely it is.

Dear Father, we know that it is You who have brought us here. We do not have adequate words to thank You. Let me not become sluggish or lazy, Lord—lax in prayer and in Your Word. It could be easy to become complacent . . . and yet . . . it seems I am communing with You all the time.

April 18, 1967

*Wait for the LORD; be strong and
take heart and wait for the LORD.*

—PSALM 27:14

Waiting *is* important. In every experience we can learn something about God. If our inclination is to hurry, or to evade the situation, we will miss God. The enrichment and revelation He had planned for us will be thwarted. Waiting is not always easy, and involves discipline. One must pull the rein tight, rather than explode in emotion.

How easy it is to give into what we are feeling at any given time. Yet, when Christ reigns upon the throne of the heart we find an inner calmness that only He can give. Though the storm is raging without, there is peace within.

I have found this truth to be real today as a new crisis appears regarding Paul's diet. With the encouragement of Frank and Chris, who is a nurse, we will try the juicer again.

I remember, "They that wait upon the Lord shall renew their strength."

*Lord, I'm weary—Paul is weary—but we wait for You.
I look to you for strength and wisdom concerning Paul.
Please strengthen him, O God. I wait on You.*

 *April 20, 1967*

*It is good to praise the LORD and make music to
your name, O Most High, to proclaim your love
in the morning and your faithfulness at night.*

—PSALM 92:1-2

Through this scripture, Lord, You are teaching me that
I am to remember Your faithfulness and loving kindness at
all times. I know You are teaching my heart to sing, and
my lips to praise You, no matter my circumstance. You are
taking me on a long, difficult journey; a journey into
praise. I am beginning to realize this is a realm about
which I know almost nothing. You are giving me Your
songs to sing—songs in the night.

Though I feel depleted, I focus on You and try desperately
to give You my praise. It seems I can do nothing less at this
time; that I must have the right perspective when it comes
to You, Lord, in order to live as I should in this difficult
situation. I am reaching out for Your direction. I am
reaching out for Your loving hand.

*Blessed Lord, You will have to sing Your songs
through me—for I have no songs of my own. I will
give myself to You, Lord, but the music must be Yours.*

April 21, 1967

*"Because he loves me," says the LORD, "I will rescue him;
I will protect him, for he acknowledges my name. With
long life will I satisfy him and show him my salvation."*

—PSALM 91:14,16

Yesterday Paul and I went to see our Kerrville doctor.
He was kind, as always, and made a few helpful
suggestions regarding diet.

Today Kathy and I went to James Avery's craft shop
where I bought Paul a beautiful silver cross. It is a gift of
my love to him—a reminder of our Savior's greater love.
Paul was so pleased and said he never wanted to be parted
from it.

His courage, faith and love for God, and for me, fill
our lives with joy. There is a certain holy peace, in spite of
the human anguish we are sharing. God often gives
compensations. Perhaps through these difficult days Paul
and I are experiencing a more fulfilling love than some
couples know in a lifetime.

While writing in my journal tonight, I heard the lonely
hoot of an owl, somewhere out in the hills. Paul, lying in
bed in the next room, heard it also and called it to my
attention. That is just about as much noise as we hear
these days!

*Thank You for the quietness, dear Lord. It is one of
Your loveliest gifts. Thank You also for the owl!*

Weeping may remain for a night,
but rejoicing comes in the morning.

—PSALM 30:5

I spent a great deal of time in prayer last night. It seemed that every negative thought and emotion was clamoring for my attention. As I prayed these thoughts receded, new assurance came, and peace filled my heart once more. My faith was kindled, and my love for Jesus grew stronger! I was able to see that my grief and pain are natural, and are no cause for guilt or self-condemnation. My joy *will* come in the morning. In the interim, He is teaching me to sing His praises by faith.

Yesterday at a retreat in Ardmore, Oklahoma, over four hundred people stood on their feet and spontaneously offered prayers in Paul's behalf. It was intercession in the Body of Christ, led by the Holy Spirit.

I am reminded of a story about Robert Louis Stevenson. He was frail and sickly as a child, and he loved to sit in the twilight, watching the lamplighter as he came up the street, lighting the lamps. One night his nurse entered his room and asked what he was doing. "I am watching the lamp-lighter punch holes in the darkness," he replied. No matter the outcome of today's prayers, holes were punched in the kingdom of darkness as a result of prayer and praise.

My God, I give You thanks.

April 29, 1967

> *The Spirit himself testifies with*
> *our spirit that we are God's children.*

—ROMANS 8:16

Our friends, Pat and Lyle Brown, drove from San Antonio today to visit us, and tonight Chris and Frank drove up the road and stopped by to encourage us. It is great to have such loyal friends nearby. I don't know how we could do this without the love and support of our friends and family—God extending His love through others.

We are discovering that the experiences and lessons we are learning at this time are not just for us, but are meant to be shared . . . sometime . . . someday . . . with others. I ponder this in my heart, not fully understanding or comprehending.

Paul is feeling much better. There is a new look of life on his face. This evening we sat on our porch and ate chop suey together. He enjoyed it, and also the fresh strawberries that are now in season. Nutrition seems to be secondary at this point—I prepare whatever appeals to him. He has gone so many days without food.

> *For every victory, my God, I give You praise.*
> *Thank You for caring for us, mere humans.*
> *Help us to know our position before You.*

In all their distress he too was distressed,
and the angel of his presence saved them.
In his love and mercy he redeemed them; he lifted
them up and carried them all the days of old.

—Isaiah 63:9

How can one read these words and not be overtaken by God's love for His people? What can I possibly add to these words?

O God! Your love for us . . . Your love for us! You are always with us, whether we see evidence of You or not. In the darkest hours You are never more present. Help me, my God, to remember this all the days of my life. As I walk through my wilderness, You are with me, as surely as You were with Abraham, as he climbed Mount Moriah with his only son, Isaac. As You were with the children of Israel, when they trudged across the desert, so You are "my cloud by day, my pillar of fire by night."

As I pass through the valley of Baca (sorrow), You make it a place of rejoicing. I come to my Marah, and find the water too bitter to drink. But as I raise my eyes, You show me a TREE. I cast it into my bitter water, and it becomes sweet.

Jesus, keep me near the Cross.

May 9, 1967

We know that we have passed from death to life, because we love our brothers.

—1 JOHN 3:14

Paul and I are sometimes overwhelmed by the love of friends and neighbors. Chris has been coming every few days to give Paul a B-12 shot, which she feels will help him. Hardly a day goes by that some of our friends from San Antonio do not drive out to the hills to see us.

Tonight the Davis prayer group telephoned us. All of them talked to us, and Paul was able to talk briefly with each one. This group has been constantly under a burden of prayer for him since they first learned of his illness. Several from the Davis church have driven to Texas, just to spend a few hours with us.

The voices of our friends tonight came over the phone to us in overflowing love. We are truly the richest people in the world! We are rich in friends . . . and rich in our Father's love. In every possible way He is showing us that He loves us, and is in the midst of our valley with us.

Lord, my heart is filled with thankfulness and praise. How can I tell You how much I love You? I am going to show it in a more practical way by getting up earlier in the morning to spend time with You . . . my Lord.

155

May 12, 1967

But he refused to drink it; instead,
he poured it out before the LORD.

—2 SAMUEL 23:16

Once again, I feel like David must have felt, when, in the heat and dust of battle, his friends risked their lives to bring him a drink from the wells of Bethlehem. He could not drink it, but poured it out as a love offering unto the Lord.

So it seems that I must offer to God all the love, prayers, gifts, and sacrifices we are receiving from our friends. We know that it is really God's Hand, extended to us through them. They are so willing to be used of Him, and that is why their gifts are so beautiful. We have nothing, yet possess everything we need. The love of our friends, as well as of our children, is of more value than gold.

This has been a good day for Paul. He has eaten well, and walked approximately a half mile this morning!

Our perceptions are being refined. Little things which once we accepted so casually, are seen now as miracles of God's grace, and cause for deep gratitude and praise.

I praise you for small mercies, little miracles.

May 13, 1967

O my God, I cry out by day, but you do not answer,
by night, and am not silent. Yet you are enthroned
as the Holy One; you are the praise of Israel.

—PSALM 22:2,3

Your heart, my God, draws near to earth, to catch the praises of Your people! When they are praising You, You are blessed and Your heart is filled with joy. I am in awe of this, that we—sinful humans—could bless God.

You are teaching me, my God, to praise You. The Holy Spirit gives me new words with which I may praise the most wonderful name of Jesus. Lord, grant that I may have increasing capacity to love You, and then, in that love, to love mankind with the same holy love with which You have loved me. I know my response in every situation should be to praise You.

What mystery . . . what untold wisdom, power, and majesty lie in Your person, O God! To know You is life eternal, and at Your right hand is joy evermore. In Your presence is fullness of joy.

May I continue to grow in my understanding of You so that I may give You my utmost praise. Please show me how to know You more . . . serve You more . . . and praise You with all my being. Amen.

May 14, 1967

You prepare a table before me in the presence
of my enemies . . . my cup overflows.

—PSALM 23:5

What a wonderful Mother's Day! Paul and I drove thirty miles today to a little church deep in the hills for worship. Paul felt he must "stand up inside" as he expressed it, to exercise his faith.

It was a delightful drive, and the worship seemed to be entirely focused on our needs. After church Paul insisted on taking me out for dinner, and we stopped at a quaint little café along the river. Paul ate a normal meal of chicken and dumplings, even taking a second helping! It began to rain while we were eating, and the café became a little sanctuary of warmth and love.

Kathy phoned this afternoon, and her voice, filled with love and faith, was another Mother's Day gift to me.

Now the sun is shining once more, and I am sitting on our porch looking out on the river, enjoying the incredible beauty of a rain-washed world. I am in awe of my surroundings and how my Lord has blessed me so abundantly.

Wash over me, O God, with Your cleansing rain.
Indeed, "my cup overflows." Thank You.

May 15, 1967

If you falter in times of trouble, how small is your strength!
—PROVERBS 24:10

Paul has had a difficult day with a great deal of pain. Tonight, and last night, he cried out to God for deliverance from his affliction. The thing he desires from me is my faith to strengthen his, as well as my praise and thanksgiving. Sometimes my heart cries out the words of the Psalmist: "How shall I sing the Lord's song in a strange land?" The children of Israel could not do it. They hung their harps on a willow tree, and by the rivers of Babylon they sat down and wept.

Then I read the twentieth chapter of 2 Chronicles. As the people of God rose to battle, they appointed singers to the Lord, to go before the army. They went forth in holy array, singing their praise to God. As they went singing, the Lord set ambush against their enemy and they became so confused they began to destroy each other. The victory of the Israelites was so great that it took them three days to carry off the spoil. How great is our God!

So I sing my love song to You, my God, because I love You. Sometimes the way before us seems so dark, but every minute of every day, dear Lord, help me to stand fast in You.

May 16, 1967

He that is slow to anger is better than the mighty;
and he that ruleth his spirit than he that taketh a city.

—PROVERBS 16:32 KJV

It is we who decide the spiritual climate we live in each day. We open the door of our hearts and minds—either to the Holy Spirit of God, or to dark whisperings of the enemy.

On this lovely morning, looking out across our river to the eternal hills, I am making my choice as to whom my companion shall be for this day. I can look at Paul's illness and succumb to sorrow, and even despair. But I choose to look to my Lord, the Author and Finisher of my faith. I shall praise Him today, for His mercy endures forever. I choose to believe God and His Word which tells me that the ultimate victory is His.

My heart is steadfast, O God, my heart
is steadfast; I will sing and make music.
Awake, my soul! Awake, harp and lyre!
I will awaken the dawn.
I will praise you, O Lord, among the nations;
I will sing of you among the peoples.
For great is your love, reaching to the heavens;
your faithfulness reaches to the skies.

Be exalted, O God, above the heavens;
let your glory be over all the earth

—PSALM 57:7-11

Amen.

May 17, 1967

For a brief moment I abandoned you, but with deep compassion I will bring you back.

—ISAIAH 54:7

Tonight, Lord, I feel that I am living in that "brief moment" when You have abandoned me! The Psalmist cried "How long, O Lord, how long?" and this is my heart's cry also. Not for myself is my heart crying out to You, but for Paul.

I am having trouble seeing . . . my perspective is twisted and turned as I see Paul's great pain. This is the part of life I don't understand. While I know in my heart that God is just and merciful, it is so difficult to see why such pain exists—and why my dearest has to suffer. It is wrenching my heart.

You also say in Isaiah 54 that, with deep compassion, You will bring your people back to you . . . with everlasting kindness, you will have compassion toward us. And again, in Isaiah 55 verse 8, You say, *"For my thoughts are not your thoughts, neither are your ways my ways."* I am taking this in with my mind, but my heart cannot absorb it.

How can it be that he could appear so much better and then once again be so miserable and sick? Are you teaching us something?

Oh, let us learn quickly, Lord. Let us learn quickly. Please lessen his pain, Lord. Thank You.

May 18, 1967

*Blessed is the man who does
not fall away on account of me.*

—MATTHEW 11:6

It could be very easy for me to stumble, dear Lord, on this walk You have asked of me, and therefore miss Your blessing. Dear God, let this not be so with me. Help me to accept this cup which You have given me. I see, Lord, that it is Your nail-scarred hand which is holding it to my lips, and thus the cup which could be very bitter becomes sweet. I do not want to be anywhere other than where I am now, for You know what is best for me. Let me see Your truth, learn Your ways, and grow in You through these uncertain days.

I pray for truth and right perspective. I so need a supernatural strength right now, Lord—a power and peace that can only come from You. I am leaning on You more heavily than ever. Please support me with an even greater measure, so that I may be a strength and help to Paul.

I do not ask to see, Lord, only to walk with You. Let me please You, see You in all things, and rejoice always in Your presence.

May 20, 1967

*O Lord, open my lips, and my mouth
will declare your praise.*

—PSALM 51:15

With singing lips my mouth will praise you.

—PSALM 63:5

Last night I awakened with a thought in my mind: "walk with your mouth." It was a strange phrase, but for the rest of the night I seemed to be affirming the truths of God regarding Paul, and praising Him for those truths.

God tells us that we are to walk in perpetual praise—our lips are to continually praise the Lord Jesus Christ. Job prayed that he might not sin with his lips. And God cleansed Elijah's lips with a burning coal—a poignant picture of just how our words need to be fire-refined.

Our mouths are made for praise and we can sin against God as much when they are silent as when they are used for complaining, speaking ill of others, or even profanity.

*I know that words hold great power, and what issues
from my mouth reflects my heart. Cleanse my lips—
that I may only speak in truth and love. Forgive, O Lord,
the times my lips have sinned against You. Amen.*

 *May 21, 1967*

Submit to God and be at peace with him;
in this way prosperity will come to you.

—JOB 22:21

Apparently, this is what God is wanting me to do at this time in my life: acquaint myself with Him. Very seldom, in all of these long months, have I felt restless or dissatisfied. But suddenly, this evening, I am overwhelmed with wistfulness and longing. It is Sunday night, and I want to do something exciting and different! Since this is a journal of honesty, I must record my feelings as accurately as possible, and this is the way it is.

We have had family and friends here today. Now they are gone. Paul is asleep, and I am alone. Suddenly, I feel smothered in a blanket of loneliness. A feeling that life is passing me by makes me want to rush out and scream at the world: "See! I am alive! Let me join you!" I am being reminded tonight how many times I could have brought comfort and companionship to others in their loneliness, and in my busyness and thoughtlessness, I passed them by.

Somehow, the frog down on the riverbank is croaking too loudly tonight!

Forgive me, Lord, and help my lonely spirit, I pray.

May 22, 1967

There remains, then, a Sabbath-rest for the people of God.
—HEBREWS 4:9

Ah! How could I have ever questioned what *real* living actually is? With the morning, as happens so often, I have a fresh perspective. God's mercies really are new every morning. Now I can answer my own heart-cry of last night!

Life has not passed me by,
I am living in the midst of life—
For I have been found by Him.
Life is giving all—
Loving supremely and unconditionally.
Being poured out in love for another,
Loving not oneself—even unto death.
Life is being needed,
Loved, cared for, and cherished.

Life is tears and sorrow, heartbreak and joy.
Sharing burdens, and praying together;
Being a friend, and having them.
Making mistakes, and learning from them.
Life is loneliness and longing,
Pain and suffering, fun and laughter.
Life is achievement and disappointment,
Sunlight and shadow.

Life is dying—to receive God's greater Life.
Life is living within the shadow
Of God's sheltering love and rest.

For giving me life in all of its fullness,
For new vision and realization,
I give You thanks, My God.

 *May 23, 1967*

The heavens declare the glory of God;
the skies proclaim the work of his hands.

—Psalm 19:1

Tonight I am sitting on the porch, overlooking the river—watching another full moon as it spills its enchanting light over our world. It is very quiet, except for the customary night noises.

This has been a good day for Paul in that he has had a better appetite. But oh, how very frail and tired he is! One month ago he and I sat together under the stars and watched the moon come riding over the hills. The days go by so fast, and yet, it seems that time has stopped. We live in a world of no beginning and no ending. And always the battle to find food which Paul can eat—

But in spite of this, I lift my eyes and the heavens are declaring the glory of God and telling me that God IS. "I AM who I AM," God said to Moses. And on a night long ago, a man looked at these very heavens, and with great joy declared:

O Lord, our Lord, How majestic is your name in all
the earth . . . When I consider your heavens, the work
of your fingers, the moon and the stars, which you have
set in place, what is man, that you are mindful of him,
the son of man, that you care for him? O Lord, our Lord.
How majestic is Thy name in all the earth!

—Psalm 8:1,3,4,9

May 24, 1967

*For our light and momentary troubles are achieving
for us an eternal glory that far outweighs them all.*
—2 CORINTHIANS 4:17

We have been enjoying beautiful, warm days. Our
neighbors and friends join us from time to time and we
share our food and eat on card tables, under the trees.

It was Job who declared that, *man born of woman is
of few days and full of trouble* (Job 14:1). This certainly
appears to be true for us! Paul has been enjoying the warm
sunshine, and yesterday fell asleep in his lawn chair. Time
passed, the shade shifted, and he was badly sunburned. His
skin is very tender, and he was in great pain.

All the village stores were closed by the time the pain
became severe, and all our dear neighbors were gone. Finally,
I called Camilla Butterfield, known as the "hill-country"
angel—a true saint of God. She drove quickly over the
miles, bringing stalks of aloe vera with her. She stood for
several hours, gently applying the soothing gel from the
stalks to Paul's burning legs, and a miracle happened! The
pain subsided, and Paul slept peacefully all night.

He is much better today. I am not sure whether the
healing was a result of the aloe, or Camilla's love and
prayers. I am inclined to suspect the latter.

*Father, let Your blessing rest upon Your servant, Camilla.
Thank You for the aloe, in which You placed some of
Your healing properties. Thank You for dedicated fingers,
through which Your healing power may flow. Amen.*

 *May 31, 1967*

> *But those who hope in the LORD will renew their strength. They will soar on wings like eagles; they will run and not grow weary, they will walk and not be faint.*

—ISAIAH 40:31

Lord, I am suddenly discovering that I am very weary. You know the steps my feet must take each day—the tasks that I must do. Both the emotional and physical aspects of my situation are wearing on me, leaving me feeling low and lackluster. I know I need so much to be "completely there" for Paul in every way . . . I want that more than anything right now.

If I am going too much in my own strength, instead of Yours, forgive me! I know I must rely on You. So fill me anew with Your Spirit, Lord, so that I may do all that is required of me in Your Spirit and grace. It is such a joy and privilege, Lord, to serve You through Paul. Let it not be spoiled by carelessness on my part. I never want to have regrets because I failed in what You have entrusted to me.

Give me new energy, Lord. And, please, keep me always abiding in You. Amen.

June 1, 1967

For I am the LORD, your God, who takes hold of your right hand and says to you, do not fear; I will help you.
—ISAIAH 41:13

I am in awe at the tenderness of this verse . . . that You would lean down toward us and extend Your holy hand. Lord, I know that if You are holding my hand, I have nothing to fear. For in Your great hand is strength and life, and all that I need for each day. My heart is filled with praise even though my weariness continues. I pray for renewing energy.

Kenneth and his eight-year-old daughter, Kendell, are here today and they have enjoyed boating on the river. It has been wonderful having them with us and watching them enjoy this beautiful area in which we have the privilege of living. We selected a lounging chair for Paul and hope it will enable him to be more comfortable, especially when he is eating. Keeping him comfortable is one of our main priorities.

Thank You, dear Lord, for holding my hand today. Please remind me that You are near to those who draw near to You. Draw me near, I pray.

> *Recalling your tears, I long to see you,*
> *so that I may be filled with joy.*
>
> —2 TIMOTHY 1:4

This scripture speaks of the joy we experience when we see friends and family, especially those who are believers.

Tonight we had a prayer and praise service at our cottage. Our friends and neighbors from here and Kerrville dropped by to spend the evening. Cleo and Bill Cutler from Corpus Christi were also with us.

It was wonderful to sing the dear, familiar hymns and to worship once again with those who love the Lord. They are a salve to my wounded spirit. The fellowship was rich and we were all encouraged and strengthened. The group anointed Paul with oil, according to James 5:14, and prayed for me also. I am so refreshed and rested now that I believe my recent weariness has been more of the Spirit than of the flesh. I needed Christian fellowship, and worshipping with our friends was better than a week's vacation.

Thank You, Lord, for bringing Your children to strengthen us.
You are constantly answering my prayers in such tangible ways.
I praise You, because Your compassion never fails.

June 4, 1967

She communed with him all that was in her heart.

—2 CHRONICLES 9:1 KJV

Paul and I had a long talk today. We communicated on a deeper level of honesty than at anytime since his illness began. One of the most difficult aspects of this experience is that Paul wants me to look to God, with him, for his healing. This has been a growing experience for me, but also a most difficult one. I have felt restrained in expressing my normal fears and anxiety, lest they be misinterpreted as a breach of faith. Candor between man and wife is very important.

Together we faced the possibility that Paul may get worse. Again he asked me to support him and protect him from those who might weaken his faith. He wants me to encourage our children to trust God, and to keep reminding them of His faithfulness, no matter what comes. He also asked me to sing as often as possible, saying that it sustains and encourages him. As I knelt by his bedside, he prayed for me. He touched Heaven in my behalf. He then took my hand and assured me that the time will come when I will know, absolutely, God's will for his life.

Keep a song in my heart, dear Lord, for You and for Paul.

171

June 5, 1967

*For great is your love, reaching to the heavens;
your faithfulness reaches to the skies.*

—PSALM 57:10

God's sovereign graciousness is often difficult to fathom. I am discovering that, at times, in spite of my weakness and lack of faith, God renews me in a most surprising way—often when I am feeling farthest from Him.

As I write in my journal each night, I sometimes ask: "Lord, why have I felt compelled to keep this record for the last year and a half? Sometimes it seems rather foolish . . . especially when I am very tired." However, as I bring my weariness and discouragement to Him, I discover that this writing becomes more than keeping a journal—it is an adventure with God. I find myself looking forward to these evening meetings with eager expectation.

As I record my failures, fears, and struggles, I discover that I am also recording my small—though sometimes impressive—victories, as well as God's great faithfulness. God's love, I am learning, has nothing to do with our worthiness . . . it is unconditional! Consequently, I find at the end of each day my heart and hand joined to pen and notebook.

Accept, dear Lord, my evening songs of love to You.

June 6, 1967

And live a life of love, just as Christ
loved us and gave himself up for us as
a fragrant offering and sacrifice to God.

—EPHESIANS 5:2

I long to be this to Paul!

Dear Lord Jesus, through the years You have loved me so tenderly through this man. Now it is my desire that every word, touch, and act of service be as healing and loving as though You Yourself were ministering to him.

Is this possible, Lord? Sometimes I feel so inadequate when it comes to caring for him. Indeed, sometimes I am, especially when it comes to the pain he is experiencing. I need direction. I need endurance. I need the guidance of Your Spirit.

All day I have tried to console and strengthen him with Your Word, and tonight I read to him until he fell asleep. I have taken care of him today for You. Now, dear Lord, I commit him into the safety of Your arms, that You might watch over Him for me. This, I know, is the very best I can do for him. You love Paul much more than I ever could and You know him fully.

Please give him a peaceful night, Lord. Thank You. Amen.

He will have no fear of bad news;
his heart is steadfast, trusting in the Lord.

—PSALM 112:7

I could very easily live in fear, not knowing what the next day will bring. The illness of a loved one can place a person in an uneasy position, giving a totally changed perspective on life and carrying out the normal tasks of each day.

This scripture is a key to victory over fear. If we are honest, we must all confess to times of being afraid. The Psalmist declares fear is overcome by having a heart fixed upon God and trusting Him. "Heart" in this instance means the whole of our attention. It is a steady gaze at the one in Whom we have come to trust—born out of long association and experience.

As we come to know the character, integrity, and desirability of Jesus Christ, He will become our central focus. Perhaps such a goal cannot be perfectly attained in this life. But we know with certainty, our chief joy in eternity will be in beholding Him.

Make my heart steadfast, Lord, trusting You that I might not live in fear of the future. Thank You for Your love for Your children.

June 11, 1967

*I know, O LORD, that a man's life is not
his own; it is not for man to direct his steps.*

—JEREMIAH 10:23

A new crisis has suddenly developed, and we are faced with a decision. Due to plumbing problems here at the cottage, it is necessary for us to move. Kenneth wants us to move back to San Antonio, where we will be closer to him and Kathy. God has used Ken on several occasions to make His will known to us, so we are accepting this as God's next step. We shall begin looking for an apartment.

Sometimes God uses strange things—even a malfunctioning septic tank—to accomplish His purposes. When walking by faith, one must trust and cling more tightly to the Father's hand. Paul and I have had happy hours, as well as difficult ones, in this little cottage by the river. We have loved living here and will be reluctant to leave. But God knows what is best for us, so we are preparing to leave.

And the Lord went before them by day in a pillar of a cloud, to lead them the way; and by night in a pillar of fire, to give them light; to go by day and night (Exodus 13:21 KJV).

*Dear Father, we are pulling up stakes, preparing
to fold our tent once more and follow You.
We will follow, Lord, as You lead the way.*

June 14, 1967

Great peace have they who love your law,
and nothing can make them stumble.

—PSALM 119:165

We have been led from our little cottage in the woods to an apartment in San Antonio. As usual, God's provision is perfect for us.

We are spending our first night in our new home. Paul loves it, and we are so very happy to be near our children. I chose this apartment for its pleasant atmosphere. A large swimming pool is in the center of the complex. We are on the second floor, with a nice patio area for sunning very near our front door.

For the first time since we left Oklahoma, I feel settled. God has given us such striking contrasts: the quiet serenity of the hills, and now the bustling city with its noise and activity. It seems right to be here, and I am grateful for a loving Father who knows our needs, and how to meet them, so much better than we do. Our transplanting has been effortless . . . suddenly we needed a place to live, and almost as quickly, we found ourselves in the right place.

I am grateful, O God, and thank
You for Your perfect care for us.

June 16, 1967

O my Comforter in sorrow, my heart is faint within me.
—JEREMIAH 8:18

One has a clearer understanding of these words when the body is weary . . . when there appears to be very little light with which to walk. Today was spent getting settled—one more time. I hope we will not have to move again soon.

Today, reading the Scriptures, I came to a description of Barnabas the apostle which I believe applies also to my Paul: *He was a good man, full of the Holy Spirit and faith, and a great number of the people were brought to the Lord* (Acts 11:24). I am convinced God is accomplishing more through Paul than we can dream. This not only includes those who are close to us, but casual acquaintances as well.

He is resting tonight, peaceful and relaxed. He did not want me to leave him alone. As I knelt by his bed, I watched the beautiful city lights from our bedroom window and sang to him until he fell asleep. Down the street I could see a large, unblinking neon light. It reminded me of the all-seeing eye of God. Although we must sleep, He does not.

Goodnight, dear Lord. I love You.

June 18, 1967

Have we not all one Father?
Did not one God create us?

—MALACHI 2:10

Jesus taught us about God and uniquely revealed Him as Father—Christ's Father and our Father. How amazing that we can call the Creator of the universe "Father."

Today we honor our earthly fathers. Ken called this morning, and Jack, Kathy, and the children were here several times. Jack took the truck and went back to the hill country cottage to bring Paul's comfortable lounging chair—a loving, practical gift. We gave Paul an album of his favorite hymns. It has been an easier day for him than yesterday.

Friends came this evening and we sat in Paul's room in the twilight, talking and watching the beautiful city lights from our bedroom window. We had a quiet, enjoyable time together. Friends and family continue to be a tremendous strength to both of us.

I have so many things for which to praise You, my God . . .
but oh, how it hurts! The pain in my heart is deep. Even so,
I love and trust You, Lord. As the curtain of night falls
upon us, so my praise rises to You—my Lord and my God.

June 22, 1967

Therefore do not worry about tomorrow,
for tomorrow will worry about itself.
Each day has enough trouble of its own.

—MATTHEW 6:34

There is one thing I am learning, and it is that *today* is all we have. Each day brings its own crises, and its own blessings, and God has promised sufficient strength for that day. I must not look ahead, wondering about and fearing the future. He has promised; "as thy days, so shall thy strength be." I hold fast to this promise.

Today has been a happy, quiet day. Paul is feeling so much better . . . almost like his old fun-loving self, and was able even to tease a little. It was like former times and makes me long for him to be well again. Our friend Ervin was here today and, as always, brought God's love and comfort. To "walk with the Lord in the light of His Word" means a walk of childlike faith, even as the above scripture implies.

Thank You, Father dear, for this one, perfect day
of rest from the conflict. Help me to take one day
at a time and to serve You with every day. Amen.

June 29, 1967

This poor man called, and the LORD heard him;
he saved him out of all his troubles.

—PSALM 34:6

Ervin gave me this scripture this morning.

The enigma of human suffering is indeed being manifested in our present situation. But we know we are not unique; the world is full of pain and sorrow. Jesus said it Himself.

A storm rose on the sea of Galilee and the disciples were afraid of the waves and strong wind. We read the words in John 6, *and it was now dark, and Jesus was not come to them.* The fact is, they had lost all hope that He *would* come to them. They thought they had to ride out the storm alone. How could He find them in the darkness?

What blessed hope! He did find them . . . He did come! They saw Him walking toward them upon the waves, drawing near to their boat. And He spoke to them words of eternal truth: "It is I; do not be afraid." He *was* in the midst of the storm. Riding upon His own creation, He came to them!

He walks to us over the seas of our distress; He comes upon the winds of darkness and despair, and always the words are the same: "It is I; do not be afraid."

O Jesus! You are the light in my darkness.
You are my song in the night! Amen.

July 2, 1967

Give thanks to the LORD, for he is good;
his love endures forever.

—PSALM 107:1

This is the Fourth of July weekend. As the day began it gave every evidence of being a long and lonely one. Kathy and Jack have gone away to Houston. Paul was very quiet and slept a lot. To be quite honest, I was feeling morose about the day.

Yet, what prompted me to fry a whole chicken this morning? To what (or whom) could I attribute this culinary inspiration? *You* knew, O God, that I was not to be alone! Cleo and Bill surprised us and came from Corpus Christi this afternoon. They stayed until nearly ten o'clock tonight. How they ministered God's love to us!

Ervin and Elwood also came to see us this afternoon and brought Communion. They anointed Paul with oil and prayed for him. Then, when they had left, Corinne and Clifford came. Wonderful friends who know and love You, too, Lord.

So, once again, You remind me You are well able to supply my every need . . . even the need for fellowship. You knew how much I needed it. Now I can sleep. Thank You, dearest Lord.

July 8, 1967

Ye shall dwell in the land in safety.

—LEVITICUS 25:18 KJV

Since moving to San Antonio, I have the feeling of having at last arrived where we are to be . . . perhaps always. There is a feeling of homecoming and security. There is just something about Texas!

In my married life my roots have been pulled up many times. I have never really known the security of a permanent location for very long. This enables me to understand another aspect of our Lord's ministry on earth. It was never His home, nor did He have a place of His own to "lay His head." Heaven was His home.

Several years ago I attempted to express to Paul what our home meant to me:

> *My home is warm and safe and dear,*
> *Its walls are beautiful and fair,*
> *Life holds for me no thought of fear,*
> *Because, dear one, you are there.*
>
> *Without, life presses with fierce din,*
> *Through the mist unknown terrors rise,*
> *I close the door, and find within*
> *The tenderness that's in your eyes.*
>
> *When from these walls protecting me,*
> *I must be gone for a little while,*
> *I hurry home, again to see*
> *The welcoming light of your smile.*

Thank You for our home.

July 15, 1967

So that we may boldly say; the Lord is my helper.
—HEBREWS 13:6 KJV

I feel as though I am living in a dream world. I go about doing all the necessary things, with a heart that is crying day and night. We are making Paul as comfortable as possible. Each step we take is undergirded with prayer. Our doctor joins us in this. He is a very special person, coming by with his wife at unexpected times, sending us flowers, and most importantly—giving us his prayerful support as well as his medical knowledge.

This weekend a carload of our church friends from Oklahoma drove to see us. Their love and faith were greatly needed and certainly strengthened ours. One night we took Holy Communion together, as we have done many times in the past. Our Lord was lovingly present in our midst as He always is when His children are gathered together.

Jesus, keep my heart pure and for You only during these days. I am weak, but You are strong. Let me rise in Your strength and do . . . and be . . . the impossible for Your glory. I offer You my hymn of praise. Although the night is dark, yet "the Light shineth in the darkness." I praise You, my God, that Your Light shines in my heart. Amen.

July 16, 1967

*Do not be afraid. Stand firm and you will see
the deliverance the* LORD *will bring you today.*

—EXODUS 14:13

This is the promise given me for this heartbreaking day. At noon it seemed that Paul was going to slip away from us. In the midst of the crisis, instead of fear, I was aware of a strength that I have never before experienced. My Lord was there . . . and held me in His arms!

On their way home from church, Emily and some of her friends came by to visit. Their prayers along with ours brought added assurance that Paul was indeed in God's hands.

Paul rallied, and after a family consultation with our doctor, we brought him by ambulance to Methodist Hospital. He is now resting and being tenderly ministered to by the hospital staff. I am spending the night here, on a cot in Paul's room. He is comforted by my presence.

*My God, I thank You for the strength and peace
You have given me today. Your voice spoke "peace"
to the raging storm, and my heart is tranquil as it
rests in You. Amazing grace! Amazing grace! I stand
in awe, my Lord, before Your majesty and power.
I love You with my whole heart. Amen.*

July 18, 1967

*We have come to share in Christ if we hold
firmly till the end the confidence we had at first.*

—HEBREWS 3:14

Yesterday and today have been days of anxiety and
tension. We have gone up and down the ladder of hope
and sorrow, always ending at the top of the ladder in the
love of our Savior, knowing He is with us.

It has been a struggle getting Paul adjusted to the right
medication. Yesterday's sedatives made him irrational, so
these were terminated. I went to the hospital chapel and
knelt alone for prayer. I found myself crying . . . until
finally I fell asleep, kneeling in the pew. Sleep is what I
needed, and God gave me His own gentle sedative of
peace. Kenneth is here and brought Zana, his young
teenage daughter with him. Paul loves having her here and
his face brightens whenever she enters the room. He always
has a smile for her. They took me to dinner tonight . . . my
first time away from the hospital.

Now, sitting here beside Paul, I am reflecting on
today's scripture. I am alerted to its significance for the
present time—holding steadfast to my confidence in God.

> *Dear Father, please help me to make these long
> hours creative for You. Bring forth Your songs
> that I may sing You my praise. Amen.*

July 20, 1967

Hours spent in a hospital by the bedside of a loved one can only be described in contradictory terms. Only those who have had such an experience can understand the paradox. First of all, they are blessed hours—burned into the memory forever—because the loved one is still *here.* The hours vacillate from one emotional peak to another: from grief to joy; despair to hope; hours of anguish to time of praise.

We have nurses around the clock. I have been tired from lack of sleep and from sharing Paul's suffering. Now I can stay in his room at night and rest. We have found medication that is right for him. Our children . . . each of them . . . are a comfort to us.

I am under pressure from all sides to make countless decisions, which seem unimportant to me. The only thing that concerns me is that Paul be well cared for and comfortable.

I love the words of Your servant David, who sang: *And now shall my head be lifted up above my enemies about me; and I will offer in his tent sacrifices of joy; I will sing and make melody to the Lord* (Psalm 27:6 RSV).

Again, I offer You my sacrifice of praise this night, dear Lord.

July 22, 1967

Yet you are enthroned as the Holy One;
you are the praise of Israel.

—PSALM 22:3

These words are taken from the great Messianic psalm that depicts the crucifixion of our Savior. A portion of this psalm was quoted by Jesus as He suffered upon the cross, but it was written by the Holy Spirit, through the psalmist, centuries before.

I often wonder why I write in this journal day after day. I know it helps me, and makes concrete and real the events that are taking place in my life. But I can never put into words or in any way describe my pain as I watch Paul's suffering hour after hour. Now, I must live out all I have ever taught or professed. I am being spared nothing, nor is Paul. But when I look to the cross of Jesus Christ, I remember that out of the world's darkest hour came God's greatest blessing to mankind. It is then I am reminded that our pain and sorrow are not wasted. Something is being accomplished, greater than we can understand.

Jesus, I offer You my evening song of praise. As You draw near, I sense that there is pain in Your heart also, for You sorrow when we sorrow. You wept at Your friend Lazarus' grave, even knowing You would raise him up. I give You my praise and all of my love.

Enter his gates with thanksgiving and his courts with praise; give thanks to him and praise his name.

—Psalm 100:4

This is the Lord's Day, and it has been good! Our doctor was here early this morning and prayed for Paul. It was the best start ever for a beautiful day!

For Satan, it is of primary importance to divide and separate God's people. A number of years ago the friendship between us and some very dear friends was broken. The estrangement was total and painful. Because we all loved the Lord Jesus, and could not forget His admonition to love and forgive, we were reconciled. Forgiveness and restoration followed.

These friends drove to San Antonio, coming to the hospital to see us. They arrived at the right time today for Paul to visit with and enjoy them. The peace, joy and love experienced by all of us were beyond words. We could not give each other enough love. Around Paul's bed, one more time, the glory and majesty of God were made manifest in our midst!

He hath not dealt with us after our sins; nor rewarded us according to our iniquities (Psalm 103:10). Thank God this is so!

Thank You, Father, for restoring to us that
which had been lost and broken. Amen.

July 27, 1967

*The LORD is my shepherd, I shall not be in want.
He makes me lie down in green pastures, he leads
me beside quiet waters, he restores my soul.*

—PSALM 23:1–3

Paul whispered these words to me today after a time of extreme pain. Then, as I softly repeated the remainder of the Psalm, his lips moved in unison with mine. It is deep water we are treading these days, but we are treading. We are not submerged!

Somewhere in the shadows our Lord Jesus stands, keeping watch over His own. He will fulfill His promise and bring us safely through these waters into glory and victory. As an old hymn expresses it: "He is our mighty Conqueror, for He rent the veil in two."

My Father speaks to me:

Fear not, for I have redeemed you; I have summoned you by name; you are mine. When you pass through the waters, I will be with you; and when you pass through the rivers, they will not sweep over you. When you walk through the fire, you will not be burned; the flames will not set you ablaze. For I am the LORD, your God, the Holy One of Israel, your Savior (Isaiah 43:1-3).

I believe You, Lord. Amen.

August 4, 1967

*We have come to share in Christ if we hold firmly
till the end the confidence we had at first.*

—HEBREWS 3:14

When we have been born again of God's Spirit, something new and wonderful begins to happen in our lives. A new humanity is being formed in us. We are being made partakers of the very nature and character of Christ! This new life, born of God, is eternal and will abide forever.

I remind myself of this as I look upon Paul's body, so ravaged by disease. I must look beyond what *I* see, to what *God* tells me is true. This is not easy. But God (how I love those two little words . . . what a difference they make!) . . . *but God,* who raised His own Son from the dead, has promised that He *by the power that enables him to bring everything under his control, will transform our lowly bodies so that they will be like his glorious body* (Philippians 3:21). John, the "beloved disciple," tells us that at the present time we do not know what we shall be, except that we know *we will be like Him,* for we will see Him as He is!

*My God, I lift to You my evening song of praise.
Thank You for Your love and confidence in me
when my confidence is at its lowest ebb.*

August 6, 1967

*If you belong to Christ, then you are
Abraham's seed, and heirs according to the promise.*
—GALATIANS 3:29

This morning, while praying in the chapel, I felt a hand on my shoulder. It was Hettie Dickson, who had driven from Oklahoma with her two daughters. Before coming to the chapel, she knelt by Paul's bedside and prayed for him.

As Paul's condition appears to be worsening, I am finding a new kind of peace, for it simply means that Paul's deliverance is now nearer "than when we first believed."

Paul is not able to recognize or communicate with us now—but this does not mean that God cannot communicate with him. There is *no place* in the entire universe where our God is not present. All authority in heaven and on earth has been given into the hands of the Son of God. He promised His followers that He would be with us always.

Our Risen Lord spoke to John on the Isle of Patmos with the ringing words: *Then he placed his right hand on me and said: "Do not be afraid. I am the First and the Last. I am the Living One . . . And I hold the keys of death and Hades"* (Revelation 1:17,18). And so, I kneel tonight and hear, coming to me across the centuries, the victorious words of *another* Paul, and I am comforted.

*I praise You, My God, for the sure knowledge
given me, that whatever Paul's state of consciousness
at this time, YOU ARE WITH HIM. Amen.*

August 10, 1967

I know, my God, that you test the heart
and are pleased with integrity.

—1 CHRONICLES 29:17

Paul has been more tranquil today, but still somewhat irrational. How very helpless he looks, wrapped in his silent world of pain and isolation. He is in a realm now where even I, who love him so much, cannot enter.

There is within every one of us a "holy of holies" where only God can penetrate. In a very great measure Paul has withdrawn from me. We who were once so close, united as one, made so by God, are now walking separate paths. I, encompassed by bewilderment and sorrow, grope helplessly for answers. There comes a time in every person's life when he must walk alone with God.

I recall a time when a friend was facing surgery. She was frightened, and asked me to stay with her. I went to her room on the morning of the surgery, stayed with her until the orderlies came with the stretcher and walked with her down the hospital corridor. But there came a point beyond which I could not go. My friend went on alone. Paul has stored many rich hours of fellowship with Jesus. They are friends. In that shadow-world where Paul is now waiting, Jesus will come to him.

My God, help me to love and trust You,
even in that which I do not understand.

August 11, 1967

*My grace is sufficient for you, for
my power is made perfect in weakness.*

—2 CORINTHIANS 12:9

Paul's natural strength is diminishing. He is not so restless now, and he has slept much of the day, locked in another dimension—one I cannot penetrate. It's so unnatural for me not to be able to commune with him as we've done on so many occasions in the past.

Last night I left the hospital and drove to Kathy's to spend the night. As I drove through the darkened streets I sobbed, in total abandonment to my grief. The walls of restraint imposed on me for Paul's sake all of these months were broken at last. Kathy met me at the door and guided me to the porch swing where I sobbed myself into exhaustion. Kathy comforted me as only she can.

Weeping may endure for a night, but joy comes in the morning. I see no joy in the immediate, and I believe God understands my sorrow. He is one acquainted with grief and sorrow.

*Lord, I am desolate and heartbroken. Yet will I praise You,
my God. My Rock. Please make Your strength sufficient for me.*

August 17, 1967

> *Now we see but a poor reflection as in*
> *a mirror; then we shall see face to face.*
> *Now I know in part; then I shall know fully.*

—1 CORINTHIANS 13:12

I am sitting by Paul's bedside, writing in my journal. The nurse has gone to supper . . . we are alone. Outside it is raining . . . I can hear the gentle tapping of the rain's fingers on the windowpane. Inside, the bedside light casts a soft glow.

Paul is just barely breathing. Today three pastors, all from different churches, arrived almost simultaneously to pray for him. They come from everywhere . . . these dear people, who are ministering Christ's love to us. But I am numb, removed from everything except this still form lying before me. I have a blind faith. I trust my God, whom I have learned to love so much. I have served Him with joy, as I have walked by the side of this dear man God seems to be calling to Himself.

Today a beautiful thought came to me: I do not have to have perfect faith, for I have a perfect Savior. I do not have to stir up faith, or examine what I have. I have only to rest in Jesus, Who loves us both. Even now, in the midst of my deepest distress and sorrow, He gives me my song of praise and adoration for Him.

Your grace is sufficient for me.

August 19, 1967

Yea, though I walk through the valley of the shadow of death, I will fear no evil, for thou art with me. thy rod and thy staff, they comfort me.

—PSALM 23:4-6 KJV

Early this morning Paul's private duty nurse phoned me from the hospital. His breathing had changed, and she suggested I come. There was no need to hurry she said—this was just an alert. In minutes I was dressed and on my way to the hospital. A moon, almost full, was setting in unearthly beauty, even as the first streaks of dawn were tinting the eastern sky. As I drove along the quiet streets, I remembered other early mornings, similar to this one, when Paul and I had been starting on some exciting trip together.

What else happened on this, the next to the last day of my darling's life? I cannot seem to remember. All that was important was that he now had only a few more hours to travel before he entered Heaven's gate and received his Father's welcome. What weary hours these were! But Paul was almost home now, and the heavenly host must have been busy preparing him an exceedingly joyous welcome. Everything must be in shining splendor for this strong, stalwart son of God. The outstretched arms of Jesus would be ready and waiting to receive him.

Be with me, Lord. Be close.

Then I heard a voice from heaven say, "Write: Blessed are the dead who die in the Lord from now on."

—REVELATION 14:13

This day began like all the rest, yet it was different. We all knew it. This afternoon I spent what were to be my last moments alone with him . . . my beloved . . . after I had sent everyone from the room.

I talked to him as though he could hear me. I spoke of our love for each other, my pride in him, my deep gratitude for all he had been to me through the years. Standing by his bed, I prayed for him and for myself. I re-committed my life to God. I smoothed his hair, gently caressed his forehead, and touched his lips with mine.

I turned to the hospital window. A lone plane flying high against the blue of the summer sky caught my attention. Suddenly an opening appeared in the clouds as though an unseen hand was parting them. Drawn as by a magnet, the tiny plane approached the rift and entered. The clouds closed over it. The little plane was gone from my sight.

It was then I knew. A quiet peace settled over me.

At ten o'clock tonight, while Kathy and I and a dear minister friend were standing by his side, Paul's gallant spirit took its flight . . . and he was home. *Home with You, Lord.*

August 21, 1967

Do not gloat over me, my enemy!
Though I have fallen, I will rise. Though I
sit in darkness, the LORD will be my light.

—MICAH 7:8

Today we selected Paul's final resting place. The Lord had a special spot reserved for His faithful servant—a place he would have liked. In a certain area of the cemetery there was a space available at the foot of a large stone cross. The cemetery is located north of San Antonio, on the way to the hill country. The hills we love so much are all about us. Gnarled live oak trees shade the park and it will be there, tomorrow, that Paul's earthly body will be laid to rest.

Paul would have loved this place. It is beautiful, quiet and restful . . . far removed from the noise of the city. There are two live oaks on our lot, growing side by side. One is larger than the other. I leaned against it and was comforted. The trees remind me of Paul and me. The setting reminds me also of what the Cross has, and will, eternally mean to us.

There is a deep stillness within me. I cannot seem to feel anything, except the awareness that there has been an amputation. Half of me is gone. I think I must be under God's anesthetic.

Thank You, dear Lord, for Your loving care. Amen.

# *August 22, 1967*

I am the resurrection and the life. He who believes in me will live, even though he dies; and whoever lives and believes in me will never die.

—JOHN 11:25-26

Memories of this day:

Last moments alone in the mortuary with the face of my beloved husband before me . . . his thin hands clasping his worn Bible and the silver cross I gave him this summer.

The joyous memorial service—just as Paul would have wanted, at Ervin Veale's Marbach Christian Church. Brother Bill Guild's powerful prayer at the conclusion of the service, giving thanks to God for the life of this godly man.

Then the ride . . . the long . . . slow . . . quick . . . ride to the cemetery. A single rose placed on the casket. Friends, from many places, standing around me in loving support. Then it was over—our life together.

Over, darling, until we meet again. I am happy for you. You have overcome and entered into the joy and rest you so wonderfully deserve. The dawn of your eternity has just begun. How joyous it must be for you now with the Lord you loved and served so well. How richly you deserve the blessings prepared for you. How great your gain. How unbearable my loss.

I close my eyes and pray for Your strength, dear God. Help me. Help my broken heart. Amen.

August 23, 1967

In repentance and rest is your salvation,
in quietness and trust is your strength.

—ISAIAH 30:15

I am so busy . . . I reach out . . . I do not have time to find Paul. I try to think of him; to remember the last time we really communicated with each other; to remember his words. I cannot remember, and the busyness of these hours pushes him further and further away. I clutch at memories, only to find thoughts of nurses. Hospital routines. Pain. Heartbreak. Confusion.

Today I drove to the cemetery to find quiet and to collect my thoughts. As I was standing there, I thought about the women going to the tomb of Jesus, only to find it empty. And the two angels said to them: *Why do you look for the living among the dead? He is not here; he has risen!*

My God, I thank You that Paul is alive and well tonight. Freed from all the encumbrances of the flesh, he is now rejoicing in Your presence. I praise You for the knowledge that he will never be sick again! His tears have all been wiped away by Your dear hand. I am sure he is singing now, the little chorus he loved so well: "It will be worth it all when we see Jesus." Now he can sing: "It is worth it all!"

And a little child will lead them.

—ISAIAH 11:6

Today Sherry, my eight-year-old granddaughter, gave me a gift. This beautiful gift, coming through her from my Father, comforts me and gives me direction. She told me the story she learned at school of "Little Half Chick," a poor barnyard fowl which was only a half!

In some mysterious way, this sensitive child was made aware that I now resemble this unfortunate chick. She understands that half of me is gone. It seems that after many trials and misfortunes, Little Half Chick ended its life as a weather vane on the very highest steeple, giving directions to travelers in all kinds of weather.

As Sherry softly told me the story, I realized that God was speaking to me through this child. My life is not over—there *can* be usefulness and purpose . . . even for me . . . who am only half. In that moment, a prayer was born in my heart—a prayer that I might be a weather vane for God . . . sensitive to the winds of the Holy Spirit . . . pointing the way Home to Him.

Lift me, my God, out of the desert of my numbness into the aliveness of a deeper love for You. Let the chords of my soul vibrate once again with the melody of adoration and praise.

August 26, 1967

But rejoice that you participate in the sufferings of Christ,
so that you may be overjoyed when his glory is revealed.

—1 PETER 4:13

Rejoice . . . . When one is in the midst of loneliness
and grief, it is difficult to think in such terms. But as one is
willing, grace is given.

Paul was an overcomer. Early in our marriage he
became ill. We were advised by physicians to leave Indiana,
our home state, and move to Texas. We left family and
friends, and the security these provided, for an unknown
future. In a warmer climate, over the years, his health was
restored. He was aware that he was living on God's time.

Paul overcame personal wounds and rejections from
his childhood. On more than one occasion he experienced
betrayal by those close to him. During his years in ministry
he was rejected by some of his peers; this sorrow went
deep. It is difficult for those with just an intellectual
concept of God to understand one who has had, to
paraphrase John Wesley, a "heart-warming experience"
with God.

Those who love God intensely often experience
resentment and rejection from others. Paul was not perfect,
but his love for Jesus Christ was as total as I have seen. He
loved Him . . . even "unto death."

Thank You, God, for the privilege of
being married to this beautiful man.

August 29, 1967

Forgetting what is behind . . . I press on toward the goal.

—PHILIPPIANS 3:13-14

Today I took my first faltering steps back into life. I drove to Camp Christian, in the Hill Country, to the Family Camp Conference. My friend Corinne went with me.

Last week, within hours after Paul was gone, Ervin Veale almost commanded me to come. Ervin has been director of this conference for many years. My heart cried out in protest against coming, for this is one of the most difficult places I could be. Many dear memories are associated with this spot—where Paul and I lived for five wonderful years, while he managed the camp. He preached in the little church in the nearby community of Center Point, and it was there that he was ordained.

When we drove onto the grounds, I was met by waves of Christ's healing love, coming to me through my friends. My dear pastor friend, Don Hurley, ministered God's Word to me. My brothers and sisters in Christ stood about me in prayer today. Emotionally, I am bruised as though stoned, but I am confident that through the prayer and support of my friends I, like the apostle Paul, will be able to "rise up, and come again into the city."

I give You thanks, my Father, for these Your children, whom You have sent to minister Your love to me.

August 30, 1967

CAMP CHRISTIAN

" . . .The kingdom of heaven is like the
owner of a house who brings out of his
storeroom new treasures as well as old."

—MATTHEW 13:52

Today I walked the lovely, familiar hills and trails of
Camp Christian.

I went alone, remembering the years Paul and I walked
them together, being thankful for the hours we had shared.
I made myself look at the old landmarks. I climbed the
narrow, rocky trails, stood on the Vesper Ledge, looking
down on the valley far below. The sheep were still grazing
peacefully, as though they had never moved.

I wandered along the river, past the spot where we
sometimes had early morning cookouts, and I sat on the
root of the old cypress tree, which jutted out into the river.
Here I often had my early morning quiet times. I looked
up at the blue sky overhead, and realized I was not crying.
A quiet peace was beginning to creep into my heart—
God's healing love was at work.

Ervin asked me to give the Vesper talk tonight, and I
found I could do it—without tears! I used the scriptures
that have become so meaningful to me during these last
few days.

*I lift up my eyes to the hills—where does my help
come from? My help comes from the LORD, the Maker of
heaven and earth* (Psalm 121:1-2).

203

August 31, 1967

CAMP CHRISTIAN

Let us fix our eyes on Jesus,
the author and perfecter of our faith.

—HEBREWS 12:2

These instructions are worthy of my deepest attention lest the waves of the future overwhelm me.

I continue to be strengthened today by the stirring challenges of the speakers at the conference. I am also feeling strongly supported by the love and faith of those who are attending. There is neither pity nor sympathy here to pull me down, only a steady pointing to Jesus, who is my Way. I am also feeling their faith in me, when I myself have very little at this point. This, I believe, is very important for anyone going through any type of crisis. There is tremendous therapeutic value in knowing our friends and peers are expecting success, rather than failure.

I can see that even with God to help me, the kind of future I shall have is really up to me. I can bog down in a quagmire of fear and sorrow, and become a recluse, filled with self-pity. Or, I can go forward and trust God to lead me.

Father, I hear Your challenge to me today. I give
You my heart, Lord, and say with Your servant Joshua,
"As for me and my house, we will serve the Lord." Amen.

September 1, 1967

*Mary has chosen what is better, and
it will not be taken away from her.*

—LUKE 10:42

Decisions are already being presented to me. Mary of Bethany, according to our Lord's words in this scripture, made a correct decision. I hope to do the same.

My hill country friends have urged me to come back. The church Paul pastored is without a minister, and they unanimously voted to ask me to fill in until a new minister can be found. This moves me deeply. It would appear to be a beginning for me, a way of serving God and having financial security. However, I know I must not be pressured into choosing the good and miss God's best.

I cannot walk in Paul's footsteps, nor can I do his work. Going back does not seem to be God's answer for me. I seem to hear Him say, "Go forward." I must follow Christ now, for my own life, make my own "footprints in the sand." I need time to put my roots down, learn to live alone with God as my companion, and be guided by His will for my life.

*I hear You speaking to me, Lord, through Your word.
I trust You, Lord, and I respond to Your call.
Where You lead, I will follow.*

Praise be to the LORD, for he has heard my cry for mercy.
The LORD is my strength and my shield;
my heart trusts in him, and I am helped.

—PSALM 28:6,7

I look to this verse for strength. There seems no end to decisions that need to be made. We will soon have my apartment ready. When all the preparation is over I will suddenly realize that Paul is really gone. At present I cannot comprehend it.

Part of my activity has to do with Paul's memorial fund. A week before his death, I spent the night with friends near the hospital. For the first time, I acknowledged that God might be preparing to call Paul home. With the thought came the suggestion to start a memorial fund to be used for spreading the gospel to areas of great need, not necessarily those sponsored by the organized church. This would be something very close to Paul's heart.

The day after his memorial service I wrote a letter telling of Paul's death and the memorial fund. It was copied and sent to the hundreds of Paul's friends. I have been amazed at the response. Hundreds of dollars have been given, and the amount is growing each day.

I pray that many will come to know You, Lord,
through this fund. Please give me wisdom with all
of the decisions that need to be made. Thank You.

September 4, 1967

Blessed are they that mourn: for they shall be comforted.
—MATTHEW 5:4 KJV

This is Labor Day. I went to my apartment today, continuing all of my preparations to move into a new place—literally and figuratively. Jack and Kathy cleaned their garage, and in the process we went through old pictures and relics. I found many things belonging to Paul: his reading glasses, gloves stuffed in his overcoat pocket, socks in a pair of old shoes; his sermon notes, baptismal records, etc. Memories that bless and burn.

Can it be true that he is gone, or will I awaken and find it all a dream? Even though friends and family have been supportive and close, I never have experienced such profound loneliness. I came back to Kathy's tonight. It hasn't seemed the right time yet to spend my first night alone. But the time is drawing near.

Dear Father, I sing You my love song tonight,
grateful that Paul does not have to wear glasses anymore.
Nor does he have pain or sorrow. There is only joy for
him now, because he is with You! Be near to me, Lord.

*Who comforts us in all our troubles, so that
we can comfort those in any trouble with the
comfort we ourselves have received from God.*

—2 CORINTHIANS 1:4

As I emerge from months of weariness and stress, I am
learning to be patient with myself, as I would be with
another person in similar circumstances. At the beginning I
felt guilt when tears came, condemning myself as a weak
Christian with very little faith. Then I remembered Jesus
had compassion on the widow of Nain who lost her only
son. He wept at the tomb of his friend Lazarus, even
knowing He would raise him from the grave.

I am beginning to realize that our Lord understands
our grief, that He is touched by it. I am learning to turn to
Him quickly when the waves of grief sweep over me. The
sooner I turn to Him, the sooner the pain is gone.

Today I bought groceries and took them to the
apartment. It was hard to do, and I brushed away tears as
I selected food. Perhaps tomorrow is the day for me to
begin my new life.

*O God! Let me learn . . . let me grow. May I not miss
what You have waiting for me because of looking back.
Let me find Your best, Lord, not just the good. Amen.*

*The LORD will watch over your coming
and going both now and forevermore.*

—PSALM 121:8

This is God's promise to me tonight as I spend my first night alone in my apartment.

This is a strange, quiet world . . . I seem to have no feeling. Is this comfort or numbness? I am not afraid, nor am I lonely in the way I thought I would be. I feel protected and safe. As I look around my apartment, I find myself being grateful. It will be very comfortable when I get it in order. I hope to find guidance and needed answers as God and I live here together.

Memories rush and crowd, when I let them intrude into my mind. I find myself reaching back for the memories, fearful lest I should lose Paul, and the dearness of him, in the busyness and adjustments of these days. The prayer of David becomes mine tonight:

Show me the path where I should go, O Lord; point out the right road for me to walk. Lead me; teach me; for you are the God who gives me salvation. I have no hope except in you . . . He will teach the ways that are right and best to those who humbly turn to Him. And when we obey Him, every path He guides us on is fragrant with his lovingkindness and His truth (Psalm 25:4,5,9,10 TLB).

Thank You, Lord.

September 7, 1967

*You have granted him the desire of his heart and have
not withheld the request of his lips. You welcomed him
with rich blessings and placed a crown of pure gold on
his head. He asked you for life, and you gave it to him—
length of days, for ever and ever. Through the victories
you gave, his glory is great; you have bestowed on him
splendor and majesty. Surely you have granted him eternal
blessing and made him glad with the joy of your presence.*

—Psalm 21:2-6

I read the words of this Psalm today and my heart
leaped for joy, as God made real to me their significance.
Through them God showed me how beautifully He
answered Paul's prayers. God's plan for Paul is far better
than any plan of mine. I had believed, hoped, and prayed
that his work would be here, but God's purposes are best.
In the same way, I know God's plans for me—for my life—
far surpass mine. Though I can't quite take it in at this
time, I know this is true, even if it means living without my
beloved Paul.

*What can I add to these words, my God?
For a brief moment You pulled aside the veil and
let me see Your glory and the wondrous things
You have prepared for those who love You! Amen.*

September 8, 1967

*Then Solomon said, "The LORD has said
that he would dwell in a dark cloud."*

—2 CHRONICLES 6:1

Too often we expect God to come to us in glory and a
blaze of light. We expect thundering and lightening . . . the
shaking of mountains, as at Sinai. If that would happen
then we could believe—or so we think. When God comes
to us, we often do not recognize Him. He often chooses to
come in a light that appears to us as darkness.

The light that comes to us from God is not like a
flashlight, casting its beam on the walls of a dark cavern.
His light is the illumination of the mind, and a quickening
of the spirit. In a sense the light of the Holy Spirit
accomplishes the same effect in the soul as the flashlight in
the hand of the explorer.

Even as my heart aches with loneliness for Paul, so
also does it long and hunger for a deeper fellowship with
God. At present I am not seeking answers so much as I am
seeking *God*. Suffering and sorrow are all about me. While
my widowhood is strange and difficult for me, I must
remember there are many others in similar circumstances.
My pain is not unique nor is it special . . . except to me.

*Help me, my God, to find the treasures hidden
in my darkness, awaiting my discovery. Amen.*

Whoever finds his life will lose it, and
whoever loses his life for my sake will find it.

—MATTHEW 10:39

I lost myself, Lord, to Your will when I gave You Paul. Now I know You want me to find myself in You. I want to go back tonight to the young girl I was at fifteen when I first met Paul. Who was she? What talents were hidden within her, which only You knew? Have I fulfilled them? Or is there more?

Help me, from this time forward to place my needs before You—but never tell You how to fill them. As I find my own true security in You for the future, my children will be released to find their lives also. We must always keep wide spaces between us, not clinging or demanding, never manipulating. I must be what I must be, and this will please and glorify You. It doesn't matter, Lord, whether the world knows who or what I am . . . all I will ever be is what I am in Your eyes.

Are You asking me what is my soul's desire? So long I have known! It is to express You—my beautiful Savior—first with my life; then by words, written or spoken. I belong to You, Lord.

September 28, 1967

Yet I am always with you; you hold me by my right hand.
You guide me with your counsel, and
afterward you will take me into glory.

—PSALM 73:23-24

This is my hope and my prayer! From a purely human standpoint, the road before me looks long—and very lonely. There are times when I feel empty, useless . . . full of longing for Paul. I can begin to sink into a state of desperation.

Then I remember that life is over all too quickly, and my true happiness will only come as I am about my Father's business. Deep within me is the knowledge that I shall never be content nor fulfilled until I too learn to be an overcomer. I am discovering aspects of myself that I could only know through my present circumstances, and for that I am thankful. The pain is no less difficult, but I find comfort in discovery and seeking my purpose.

Dear God, guide me with Your counsel. Direct my footsteps,
and at the end of my life may I be found worthy to stand in
Your holy presence. Help me to love You as You deserve
to be loved . . . as I long to love You. Help me also
to know better how to receive Your love. Amen.

October 14, 1967

> *Simon Peter answered him, "Lord, to whom*
> *shall we go? You have the words of eternal life."*
>
> —JOHN 6:68

I went to the Waco conference feeling as though I were drowning in my tears. There had crept into my consciousness feelings of self-condemnation with the insidious suggestion that if only I had more faith Paul would be alive. Each day became worse. I wondered why God had brought me there.

On the last night of the conference we had a communion service. Absorbed in my own thoughts, I was not listening. Suddenly the speaker's words penetrated my consciousness. He asked: "Sometimes God trusts *some of us* with the unexplainable. Do you love Jesus enough for that?" Then to my own heart it seemed Jesus was saying, "*Do* you love me enough—even for this?" Not caring what anyone thought, I found myself kneeling at my seat, convulsed with sobs. This time, they were tears of release. My heart was responding: "Jesus, I *do* love You enough!"

I am now back in San Antonio. My sorrow does not seem to be any less, but there is no anguish, nor torment. I am at peace.

October 18, 1967

Come with me by yourselves to
a quiet place and get some rest.

—MARK 6:31

Today I went to Camp Capers, an Episcopal retreat center in the hills, for a quiet day of prayer and meditation. I spent my time alone walking.

It was a perfect day. The October sky was a cloudless blue, silhouetted by the many trees scattered about, dressed in their fall colors. Pieces of the puzzle, which came into focus in Waco, began to fall into place. I am sure God has many things yet to teach me, and today was a beautiful start.

Today I came to life . . . *real life* . . . for the first time in months! I *live once more.* I am alive . . . and thankful to be alive.

I give You thanks for the love that has burst into flame on the altar of my heart. For so long the fires have been smoldering, there were only a few live coals among the ashes. I have been frozen and cold, unresponsive to You. Now, my heart feels like an ice jam in the frozen northland, suddenly breaking loose when the spring thaw comes.

And Father . . . for whatever reason Paul was
called Home to be with You . . . I am thankful
I had such a beautiful gift to give You!

215

October 22, 1967

Whoever believes in the Son has eternal life.
—JOHN 3:36

All that is required for this promise is belief—belief in the Lord Jesus Christ as our Savior and God's Son. But on that little word—*belief*—hinges our destiny. For to believe that we need a Savior, and to make Jesus Christ Lord of our life, means dying here, to the life of self.

No one wants to die, not even to our lower nature— that part of us which causes so much trouble. Consequently, the conflict within us is often intense and very difficult. Our eternal destiny is the issue. Every person, at some time in his life, has to give his own, personal answer to the question Jesus posed to His disciples: "But who do *you* say that I am?"

However, our Lord gives us tremendous assurance: *I tell you the truth, whoever hears my word and believes him who sent me has eternal life and will not be condemned; he has crossed over from death to life* (John 5:24). If we are willing to die here, we shall live eternally there.

My Paul believed, therefore I need not fear for him. He passed from death to life before he left this world.

I praise You for this precious gift—too precious for words. Thank You, merciful God, for my salvation.

October 30, 1967

*I am the vine; you are the branches. If a man
remains in me and I in him, he will bear much fruit.*

—JOHN 15:5

The climb out of the valley of sorrow is a continuing experience. It is always with me. I cannot believe, even yet, that Paul is gone from me. But life continues . . . the days pass, and some have very happy moments.

The Memorial Fund for Paul has exceeded all expectations. Checks continue to arrive from friends across the country whose lives were touched by his life and ministry. From its beginning I have known the funds must go into areas of greatest need for the Gospel.

This is what Paul would have wanted. I have never had this much money to give God before! Paul's life was committed to pointing others to Christ. These gifts are a spontaneous outpouring of their love and gratitude.

Much of my time is being spent in allocating these funds. When it is finally completed, a careful report will be sent to each person who contributed to the fund. This task, during these difficult days, has been a source of great joy and comfort.

*My dear and lovely Lord, I bring this fund
to You, and place it in Your hands. Amen.*

> *Dear friends, do not be surprised at the painful*
> *trial you are suffering, as though something*
> *strange were happening to you. But rejoice that*
> *you participate in the sufferings of Christ.*

—1 PETER 4:12-13

There are times when I rejoice in the opportunity to explore the things of God in a deeper way, perhaps, than I might have in the joy and security of Paul's companionship. My need is more acute. My strength, wisdom, and security are completely dependent upon God. Looking back, I can see that prior to this time, my life had been sheltered in some respects.

Now I am being thrust forth to think things through for myself, and to make decisions on my own. It is often a strange experience. I have a feeling, if such a thing is possible, that Paul may at times look upon me whimsically—perhaps with some compassion—and I dare hope with a certain degree of satisfaction!

God, please continue to open my eyes to new things,
and give me the wisdom to think things through clearly.
I praise You that we can go on in life, even after we
experience tragedy, to learn and grow in You.

November 19, 1967

He persevered because he saw him who is invisible.

—HEBREWS 11:27

This afternoon I drove out to the cemetery. I do not do this for morbid introspection, but because it is beautiful and quiet. Also, it helped to prepare me for the Thanksgiving retreat at Palestine, Texas, where I will be one of the speakers. One year ago Paul and I were preparing to go there together. This time I go alone.

I knelt by Paul's grave and renewed my covenant with God, made on the day He called Paul home. I felt very close to Paul in spirit. The cemetery was lovely and quiet. A gentle breeze stirred the autumn flowers in the vase on the marker. After a time I leaned against the live oak tree, which represents Paul's strength to me. Looking up at the blue, November sky, I could almost feel Paul's arms around me, giving me peace and courage to go on.

I returned to the city in the gathering dusk, and went to Trinity for my second Confirmation class.

Gracious Father, I thank You for my time with Paul . . . what a blessing it is to have had him as my husband. I praise You for strength and healing. Help me to continue to look to You. Amen.

When you lie down, you will not be afraid;
when you lie down, your sleep will be sweet.

—PROVERBS 3:24

Sherry and Susan are spending the night with me tonight. How trustingly they went to sleep . . . perfectly confident in my ability to keep them safe. How I cherish them. This is the way it should be for me, too. Unfortunately, I have struggled to trust and rest in His peace.

At first, when I was alone in my apartment, I was not able to sleep. It was as though I had forgotten how to "turn on" sleep. The long nights of sleeplessness at the hospital had taken a toll and, I am certain, did not do much to help my state of mind during the day.

I am better now. It is still a strange feeling to wake up in the night and find myself alone. I sleep by the window and often, lying in bed, I look up at the night sky and remember that He who watches over Israel neither slumbers nor sleeps. I am safe in His arms. It is becoming easier.

This is my prayer: *I will lie down and sleep in peace, for you alone, O LORD, make me dwell in safety* (Psalm 4:8).

A Remembrance

When Moses went up on the mountain, the cloud covered it,
and the glory of the LORD settled on Mount Sinai.

—EXODUS 24:15,16

It is early morning in the Blue Ridge Mountains. Paul and I have been driving since before daybreak. It is extremely foggy, and we decide to pull off to the side of the road. We park our car and, walking to the edge of the cliff, peer down through the fog to the valley far below. We are above the clouds. As we stand there, they swirl about our feet and over our heads, mingling with the fog until we feel a part of them and the world seems far away. It is as if we are standing on the rim of the world at the dawn of creation.

Suddenly, the clouds part, and directly in front of us stands the dark, mysterious outline of a mountain. For a moment we can see it: strong, immovable, steadfast. Then the clouds cover it, and it is gone. After a time I became aware of tears on my cheeks. In those brief, wonderful moments, God has whispered His message to my heart: "It is like that with Me. Like the mountain, I am always with you, unchanging and eternal. Sometimes the clouds hide my face and you think I have forsaken you. But I am always there."

Amen.

About the Author

Zada E. Mitchell Sherry was born April 1, 1909, in Eaton, Indiana. She was married to Paul Sherry for forty-two years, supporting him during his long and successful business career and raising their three children. In 1956, Paul became a minister in the Christian Church, and together they pastored congregations in Texas, Oklahoma, and California.

When her husband passed away in 1967, Zada continued to minister God's love to others. She lived in San Antonio, Texas, and was a well-known Bible teacher whose love for God's Word was contagious. Zada also served as secretary to the chaplains at Santa Rosa Hospital for ten years.

Zada was an avid writer and poet, and it was her dream that this work would one day be published. It gave her great joy at the end of her life to know that she would leave a written legacy; to know that her story might bless and minister to those experiencing suffering, heartache, and grief.

When Zada realized she might not live to see this book in its published form, she said "That's OK. Paul and I will read it together in Heaven." Zada went to be with her Lord on February 7, 2001, at the age of 91. She is loved and remembered by many.

In Loving Memory

Zada M. Sherry
April 1, 1909 – February 7, 2001

Rider of rainbows,
Unconquered by storms.
An eternal crescendo,
Resonant . . . penetrating.
Spring in all seasons.

Detailed simplicity,
Intricate beauty.
Voyager, adventurer,
Singing with joy,
"Alleluia" to life!

Fabric woven of a thousand
Colors and textures.
Soft yellow sunshine;
Bold and laughing reds and blues;
Seafoam green and purest pearl white . . .
Wrought in chambers of suffering and pain.

Delicate whispers of silk,
Durable cords of wool and linen.
Pressed—but never crushed;
Perplexed—but never despairing;
Struck down—but never destroyed.

Engraved by the Words of the Master,
Soothing the fevered soul;
Bringing warmth in the midst of winter;
Enfolding the hurts of a hundred hearts.
An overcomer who walks the streets of Heaven
With Him in white.

—Kathleen Sherry Ryan

Additional copies of this book
and other titles by RiverOak Publishing
are available from your local bookstore.

If you have enjoyed this book, or if it has
impacted your life, we would like to hear from you.
Please contact us at:

RiverOak Publishing
Department E
P.O. Box 700143
Tulsa, Oklahoma 74170-0143

Or by e-mail at info@riveroakpublishing.com

visit our website at: www.riveroakpublishing.com